The Question to Life's Answers

Also by Steven Harrison

Doing Nothing

Being One

Getting to Where You Are

Steven Harrison

The Question to Life's Answers

Spirituality Beyond Belief

SENTIENT PUBLICATIONS, LLC

Grateful acknowledgment is made for permission to reproduce the
following material: Excerpts from Sustained Transcendent Experience by
Sunny Massad. Excerpts from an interview with Steven Harrison in
The Noumenon Journal, Summer, 1998, Vol. 4, No. 2. Excerpts from an
interview with Steven Harrison in Pathways Magazine, June-December, 2000,
Vol. 9, No. 3 & 4. Excerpts from an interview with Steven Harrison by
Elizabeth Gips on Changes Radio (www.changes.org), 1998.

Publisher's Cataloging-in-Publication Data

Harrison, Steven, 1954-
The question to life's answers: spirituality beyond belief /
Steven Harrison. — 1st ed.
p. cm.
ISBN 0-9710786-0-2 (pbk.)
1. Spirituality. 2. Spiritual life. 3. Mysticism. 4. Mind and body.
5. Philosophy of mind. I. Title.
291.4 — dc221
Library of Congress Control Number: 2001093071

Cover and book design by Tracy Lamb
Cover art by Robert Sturman

SENTIENT PUBLICATIONS
A Limited Liability Company
1113 Spruce Street
Boulder, CO 80302
www.sentientpublications.com

Contents

Introduction

This book is a series of explorations into how we can live. Can we live in relationship? Can we step into the unknown and construct a life unrestricted by our answers? How do we form our relationships, build our communities, raise and educate our young, care for our elders? How do we work and play? How do we address the suffering in those around us?

The answers to these questions have always brought division, because there are so many ways to answer. What if we simply live these questions? What if we hold them as the guides to our lives? What if we build our lives and our societies around discovery and exploration? What are the possibilities of a world in which the limitations of belief are recognized? Freed of the constraints of ideology, can our world, our pattern of reality, begin to restructure into something that is expressive of the unitary principles of life?

We can hardly believe that this is possible, and that is precisely what makes such a transformation a real potential. It is beyond belief. As such, this revolutionary shift of patterning is outside of the known, outside of anyone's control, outside of any power structure, outside of any one. Perhaps this life beyond belief can be touched upon with words, described in part, pointed to, or suggested. However, no one can fully explain this potential, no one can organize it, no one can guide us to it.

Our life is not a solitary life. No matter the circumstance of our existence, we live interconnected to all that is. By its nature, life is integral and collective. We cannot find our way in the unknown without each other, but together we can discover a life of passion and love, and in that discovery begin the exploration of this new world.

The Nature of the Question

THE NATURE OF THE QUESTION

The student came to the master and asked for knowledge.

"I have studied for a long time, I have read many books, and I have perfected all the practices," the student said. "I would like to know what you know."

"First, let us have tea," said the master. The master brought the pot, and placing the cup before the student, began pouring the tea. He filled the cup and kept pouring as the tea spilled across the table.

"What are you doing?" exclaimed the student.

"Oh, I see," said the master, "the cup was full. It could not hold anything else. Just like our minds—already full."

The nature of a question is the recognition that we do not know. This most basic of understandings is also the most powerful. The knowledge that trumps all other knowledge is the understanding that we have no certainty.

Not knowing allows an investigation into life that is unobstructed by our conditioning, uncluttered by our information. It is the absence of knowing that allows the discovery of the new.

What we know—the neural pathways we have assigned to a particular circumstance—patterns the experience. We fit what is new into what is old. This sorting and categorizing is a kind of intelligence and certainly not a capacity we could discard. However, as we fit what we find in life into what we remember, perhaps we can remember something else, as well—that to learn we must abandon the perspective of the past and expose ourselves to the uncertainty of what is new. This is the nature of the question.

The question is not suspicion or doubt; it is inquiry, curiosity, and openness. The past is our history, and like all history, it is distorted by the historian, which is the self that we have constructed. This self, carefully selecting from the totality of our experience in typical revisionist style, tells the fiction of our life and seeks to extend that story into each moment. This is the nature of our information and the limitation it imposes on our contact with the actuality of life. The past is illusion if it is held as an accurate map for the future.

The question does not discard the past; it integrates it. The question understands the constraints of information and seeks to expand those boundaries, perhaps even to shatter them.

The question understands knowledge as myth, a grand fable we tell to explain what we cannot really know using the tools with which we work. The great evolutionary advantage that humankind has over the rest of the animal world is not our ability to think. It is our self-awareness, the thinker turned on itself. This cognizance of our thought as representation allows us to see both thought's usefulness and its limitations.

We know that thought cannot know. Thought can only think, and therefore can only think it knows. Any aspect that thought represents cannot describe knowledge, which is inclusive of the whole picture.

Yet, we are enamored with thought because it is so apparently useful. The questioning of thought, the awareness of thought, makes its function and its actual nature transparent, and in so doing, integrates it with the perspective of wholeness that awareness carries. This integral perspective allows thought to be useful, when it is so, and refrains from involvement with thought when it is useless.

The bundling of thoughts into mind (by thought, it might be noted) gives us the sense of a center, a "me." This is the dis-integral perspective we have come to accept as the basis for our lives, upon which we have collectively shaped our society. We have accepted this "me" because we have lost perspective on the limitation of thought in representing the whole. Perhaps we have forgotten these limitations because thought is so active, our minds are so busy thinking, feeling, perceiving, sorting through all the qualities that stream through our field of awareness. Yet, however busy our minds are with this flow of information, we can never know more than what is held in that stream of data.

Perhaps the function of our mind is, as Aldous Huxley suggested, a reducing valve for the totality of the universe, a tiny scoop of reality out of the infinite everything. This is what allows us to function. Without the reduction of total input, without everything being cut down to something, we could not live.

Thought does not take this into account. Thought is convinced that its tiny piece is the infinite everything.

But thought, including the thought of the infinite everything, is just a speck in God's eye. Each of us stands in our imperceptibly tiny dab of life, asserting our separation and displaying the proof of it—our knowledge. In the flashing passage of our life, in a blink of an eye—God's eye—all that we are and all that we know is enfolded into totality, the ultimate question to all of our answers.

Losing Perspective

I saw that all my wanting, all my plans and strategies, were coming from some sort of identity. Now there is this "nothing" place, where I thought that I would be peaceful, not frustrated, because I gave up my strategies.

Where did you get that idea?

I don't know, but I want to be peaceful and do something useful with my life.

It's a big problem. Enlightened people can't do what normal people do, because it's just normal. We have to do something special! It's a real challenge.

How can I be happy? How do I find purpose in something?

The question is important. When the genie comes out of the lamp and gives us three wishes, we usually get ourselves in trouble with the first two. Then we have to use the last wish just to get our old life back. So, let us find the fundamental question. If we can answer it, we're done. But to find the answer, we have to know the question.

You've seen through the entirety of your world. You see how your mind generates ideas and plans, creates your motivation, gets you through the day. You stopped all that. Now you wonder whether your old life was better. At least you knew what you were going to do each day.

What question emerges in your life out of this circumstance?

How do I use whatever gifts I have to benefit the world, not just myself?

What to do? Is that your core question? If so, and we can create a program for you, then you're done!

I'm asking what to do, or how to live with the discomfort of not knowing what to do.

Now there are two questions. Which do you think it is? Our minds generate question after question, and then we have to answer those questions. It's a form of paralysis. This is not a questioning mind, a curious and open mind, but a mind that is generating questions endlessly, habitually, without ever getting to the core question.

Is there a deep life question? This would not be an intellectual question, but a question that fundamentally resolves something.

I just want to know what to do with my life.

Let's make sure it's the right question first. In India I went to an oracle once, one who could apparently tell the future and who was well respected for this talent. It was a long journey, and we picked up some papayas on the way so that we would have a gift for him. He was not easy to find, but after quite a bit of effort we located him. Not only that, but he was willing to see us. We were ready. We gave him the papayas. He didn't speak English, and there was no translator to be found. We had a beautiful meeting, but there was no answer to our questions. Then, as we left, it occurred to me that perhaps the meeting wasn't about our questions or his answers. Perhaps it was only about delivering papayas to the oracle. He woke up that morning, thought he'd like to have some fruit, and it occurred to us to get some fruit and bring it to him. Going to the oracle can be a tricky business.

We thought we were on a profound journey, but really we were just delivering papayas.

If I sent you to this oracle and he gave you the answer, would you act on the answer?

I would.

All right. I'll be the oracle. Go to Sacramento, and go to the WalMart located between Fifth and Sixth Streets, and get a job there. Work each day from ten in the morning to four in the afternoon. Don't work Saturdays and Tuesdays, and then wait for what is next.

Oh, God!

If this is the reply from the oracle, will you do it? Have you really understood what your question is? Is the question, "What do I do with my life?" Or is it, "What do I do that will bring me importance?" Can we understand the fundamental question if the perspective is from the "me"? Or can we understand it only from a perspective that we cannot reach with our thought, with our language, even with our intentions? If you are just the delivery system for papayas in life, is that enough for you? Or do you need to be the one who gets the papayas?

We say we want to know what to do with our lives, but why do we want to know the future? Can we know what we should do with our lives? Some theologians would say that if God sees the future, he loses some of his power, because then even God can't change the course of events.

Now, if you go to the oracle, and the oracle tells you what you should do, have you not lost something in that? Do you really want an answer to your question? You believe that if you know about the future, you will get security, you will be safe. But your life will just be a mechanical unfolding into that future. So, it's good that you didn't ask that question.

I would like to do something that I could be happy doing for its own sake. Just happy doing something joyful, something I am excited about, passionate about. Not passionate about the illusion of it, just passionate about it in and of itself.

How do you know the difference?

I don't. That's my problem! That's why I'm paralyzed.

Sometimes you're passionate and happy, but it's illusion, and other times you are passionate and happy, but it's not illusion. You would like to do the passionate and happy thing that is true, not the passionate and happy thing that is false.

Yes.

What criteria do you use to make that true/false judgment? What is it that judges?

Maybe passion has nothing to do with illusion or truth. Maybe it was just what it was in a moment. In hindsight, when I did not have it anymore, I decided it was an illusion; therefore it was all false.

Why do we give happiness over to unhappiness to be the judge? What is it that is choosing the perspective?

Since happiness seems to be built on so much illusion, I don't trust it.

Why do we trust this unreliable thing called "me" to tell me about happiness? When you are happy, there doesn't seem to be any problem. But you have the idea that happiness is not all right, because it is built on illusion.

The question that we've discovered is not about whether happiness is real or what to do about happiness. It is about the perspective that's analyzing, judging, creating, or uncreating happiness. Is this perspective real? Is it reliable? This is the perspective out of which we are trying to live.

Perhaps this is the question in the end: "What is it out of which I can live?"

I never saw it that way, but yes. When you feel happy, you feel happy.

How else can you feel? When you're happy, you're happy; when you're angry, you're angry; when you're unhappy, you're unhappy; and on and on. How else would it be? You understand your whole reality through this perspective. But what is this perspective?

My identity is about ambition, wanting to be somebody who makes a difference in the world. All that is wrong. That is my mind rather than the truth of being in a moment.

So, all those things are wrong from the perspective. Then, what is right?

That's the problem.

What does the perspective say?

Be in the moment, and allow whatever is to be.

That's interesting. The perspective is suggesting that you have a choice. You can either be in the moment and leave things as they are, or you can...do what? Where else can you be, besides in the moment? What else can things be other than as they are?

They can't, really.

The perspective has to be suggesting some alternative, or there is a logical fallacy. There's another part of the message that is implied. What is the rest?

That if I'm pursuing something, I'm not in the moment and that is wrong.

Is that true? Where are you when you are pursuing something? I would like to go with you to a place that's not in the moment. Then we can tell whether this perspective is correct. Where is it? Why is it wrong? If we cannot find this world outside of the moment, then it seems to me that this perspective is a tormentor that is saying that everything you actually are is wrong. What can you do with the perspective that says, "Everything I am doing is wrong"?

It really leads to paralysis.

You're supposed to be doing what is right, but everything you do is wrong. It's easy to see why you're confused! Where did the perspective come from, and what are we going to do with it? Shall we send it back to hell, where it came from?

If for one moment, the perspective falls absolutely silent, what happens to your life? What happens to your doing, your ability to function, your happiness?

I've decided so much from this perspective. I don't know what to do without it.

Why do you have to decide? Has the perspective found its way back so quickly?

So, how do you not decide about anything?

What is not deciding?

Just doing nothing.

You're in a state of confusion because the perspective is just a set of rules. Your perspective and mine are different. You grew up in a different way, you read different books, you went to a different school, had different experiences. I have to apply my perspective, which is conditioned, to that.

The perspective tells us, that's the right thing to do, or that's the wrong thing. And without it, what happens?

The perspective says to us happiness is false and whatever you are is wrong. Why do we need that? Without a perspective, aren't we inherently happy? There is no commentary to tell us we are not. We are left with "what is." We are led by what interests us, what energizes us, what fulfills us.

I'll let go of the perspective.

How do you let it go? Do you trick it? Send it in the wrong direction?

Is this perspective just my thoughts?

Yes. You know what you're interested in. This perspective is commenting on that, constantly telling you that whatever you are is wrong.

Everybody's mind does this; this is not just me.

This is the nature of psychological thought. It's the accumulation of all our collective, cultural conditioning. That's what we bring into every experience. That's why our experience is so cluttered and dissatisfying, because we're not having experiences, we're having thoughts. This is what our reality is, the chattering perspective. We don't smell a rose, we comment on the smell of a rose. If we could smell a rose, it would be nice.

Without the commentary, what is there to do?

Are you without a commentary?

I would like to be.

This is a lovely story. Without this perspective, everything will taste better, look better. Life is great without the perspective.

That's what I think!

And, that is what it is—a thought.

You're saying it's not true?

What's true is that we have a perspective, a running commentary, but instead of making full contact with the perspective, we let ourselves be tricked. The commentary said to us that there's a really great place outside of this perspective, so don't look at the perspective.

In actuality, the perspective is where you are. Can the perspective see itself?

If I could separate myself from it, I could see it. But I can't, because I create the perspective.

Is there anything that can apprehend the perspective?

Lately, I've been having dreams where I feel awake in my dream. In other words, I'm aware that I'm dreaming.

You're awake to your dream. You're aware that the dream is only the perspective, or should we say the perspective is only a dream. Is there something that's awake while we're in the dream of our perspective? In this moment, are you awake to the dream? Are you aware of the nature of the perspective, the mechanical nature of the self? Now awareness takes over the dream. You're awake, but that awakening is not the bundle of tendencies, conditionings, and habits of the perspective. Your life is directed by something else. We don't know much about what that means, because what is known is held by the perspective, what is unknown is held by awareness. What we're left to do with our life is to inquire into this unknown space of awareness. And this life of inquiry is a rich and full one.

Exploration and Beingness

Have the words "consciousness," or "awareness," or "emptiness" become synonymous with a more sophisticated sense of a personal me?

Indeed. We are not just paltry, confused thinkers any more. We are not even desperate spiritual seekers trying to cultivate awareness or experience emptiness. Now we have traded it all for consciousness. We are that! We can relax. We still have an identity, and a big one, at that. We've filled the emptiness once more.

Is there consciousness without thought, symbol, sound, or image? In a state of being such as sleep, are all these qualities passive? During sleep there is no me. As soon as I wake, my state seems to undergo a change much like that of ice changing to water. Could you please explain what you mean by "consciousness"?

I am using the word "consciousness" to mean the field of awareness in which everything that we apprehend arises and passes away. Neither science nor philosophy has really come to grips with what consciousness is. We can see some of the effects of consciousness, much as we can "see" the wind rippling the water of a lake. We can say, perhaps, what it is not, such as thought looking at thought, the watcher—a kind of facsimile of consciousness cooked up by thought. But the question of what consciousness is, is a profound question. We must hold it as a question and thereby outside of the known, if we hope to discover anything about it.

By holding the question as a perspective, do you mean exploring without reaching a conclusion? What is the difference between exploration and seeking?

The sense of seeking often has the quality of something missing and with that, a projection of what completion would look or feel like. Carrying this template with us as we seek, we look for the parts or states that we imagine we need.

The sense of exploration is not really about acquisition at all. It is naturally interested regardless of what it discovers or doesn't discover. This is possible only when the exploration comes from a perspective of wholeness, as the fragmented perspective will generally turn the whole thing into seeking.

Aren't we after an impersonal "I" that is not "I" at all, but is all that is, as it is, including all thoughts, feelings, and actions—excluding nothing, controlling nothing, changing nothing?

We already have all that is, as it is. Part of that "as it is" is that we are constantly struggling with our thoughts, feelings, and actions, and we love to exclude things we don't like, control anything we can overpower, and change whatever we can manipulate. The "as it is" is painful. We want a better "as it is," the kind described in the spiritual literature. In the mythology of spirituality, "as it is" is a code word for the bliss of non-attachment. This spiritual fantasy would be more accurately described as "as it isn't." I don't think there is any school of spirituality that is about achieving life "as it isn't," though. That probably wouldn't market well.

I seem to have awakened from the conceptual world, and now stand outside it, yet fully accept it. But last night I found myself reacting to my partner with a strong sense of self and disturbance. This morning it has disappeared, and the feeling of living from awareness and not-self is back. What is going on?

Is this sense of self-identification related to a feeling of being threatened? Is it related to preservation?

Thought seems to have evolved as a technology for survival. In the conceptual world, survival of the psychological "me" has taken on a false importance and a virtual reality. Now, when my partner signals that his or her affection or attraction is not consistently there for me, it's as if my concrete life is at stake. My identification solidifies. I survive even at the expense of destroying the intimacy of the relationship. And yet, there was never a real threat outside of the imagined world of the psychological self.

Perhaps what is most interesting is a relationship that embodies the understanding of this movement to self and the release back into intimacy. This relationship is neither destroyed by the appearance of self nor enamored by the apparent absence of self. This relationship is inherently whole even as the movement of thought arises and passes away, even as the sense of self and selflessness comes and goes.

Will the coming and going of a sense of being without the self eventually stabilize as a simple functioning from awareness?

Perhaps the sense of self will never be gone, based as it is in biology, physicality, social contracts, and the need to constantly locate ourselves to navigate our day-to-day lives. However, the perception of the conceptual nature of self totally alters it. There is not a "me" or a "not-me," but simply the arising and decaying of thought in the vastness of silence. We are all that.

What does it mean to truly see "what is," or to observe?

Observation is the state of being, rather than any act of doing, however insightful. Observation does not stand back from life but is merged with it. This beingness is the actuality, including the fact that the mind, addicted to its attempts to model and manipulate the world for its own survival, continues to ramble on.

There is often the projection of a non-thinking, or at least relatively quiet, mind as a result of our observation. But thought forms as it does, and any effort to change it is simply subsumed into a more complex and subtle mental framework.

The "me" cannot go beyond itself, because it has no actuality outside of the concept that it is, and that it can go beyond. The only thing the "me" dominates is the world that it has thought of and structured so that it can stay in control. This is a mere fragment, swallowed up by the vastness of the actual.

Perhaps we're concluding that by observing the absurdity of our suffering we might detach from it. Then the chattering mind might subside, and we might start to see and feel the beauty all around us, and be in that perfect stillness without thought intruding.

The idea of detaching, and thereby diminishing the thought world until we achieve silence, is not the answer to the absurdity, it is the absurdity itself. What if the thought world exists without us doing something with it such as detaching, diminishing thought, or achieving silence? What if we do nothing with the thoughts as they occur? It is not the thoughts that are the complexity, but the attempt to sort them, control them, organize them, focus them, refine them, avoid them. Without the doing—the attempt to change all of this—we are naturally left with being in the world-as-it-is.

I suppose what I find troubling is the alternating sense of vastness, and all the creativity that arises out of it, and the limited constrictedness, which I find is really a state of fear. And then all the thoughts about how to deal with fear, the biggest thought being that I should simply witness it all.

Try being the fear as it arises. This immersion in the actuality is very different from the "standing back from it" quality that is brought about by witnessing. This is the collapse of the divided world of consciousness and object into a world where consciousness and object are one. This seems to be where the discovery of the wholeness of life takes place, in the totality of being, whether we experience so-called positive or negative qualities.

What would you say your "state" is like? Obviously the relationship to thought is different because you seem to suggest that there is no feeling of division.

There's a full range of feelings and qualities. But where is the center? There's no fundamental difference between my state and yours, or anyone else's, for that matter, simply because we are all the same field of consciousness/thought, and only divided conceptually, not actually.

My state is like a moment. It is not much different from a young child asking me to tell him a story. I tell him a story, and we both know that it's both momentarily real and unreal. We enjoy the story immensely. Then the story is over.

If indeed there's "nowhere to go" and "nothing to be," then why the vigorous exploration into the nature of life? Is your exploration aimless? Mine doesn't seem to be.

Our language is built around subject-object and noun-verb structures. We ask how there can be a subject without an object, or whether a noun without a verb is really a sentence. But life is not language, and it isn't limited to those structures.

There does seem to be exploration in our lives, but why does that require a psychological center? Indeed, the exploration of life is possible only when the limitations of the conceptual world are obvious. This transparency of thought, which implies a thinker but doesn't possess one, leaves us in a universe where it appears that the space around thought is now the foreground, and the thought-form is the background. On closer examination, even the distinction of foreground and background disappears. We are left where there is only one thing happening, which can neither be described as subject nor object, noun nor verb.

What is this world? The inquiry has started. There is no one to ask or answer, and the questions aren't verbal or intellectual anyway. The inquiry is the movement of life.

I wonder what role the body has in your work. It seems to me that the body and brain are very much like a web browser (or vice-versa). That is, the body contains one's individual awareness and "manages" the exchange of data between the "user" and physical reality.

On a practical level we have to take care of our bodies, or they will get sick, die, or otherwise become problematic. Is there a body there at all, in a discrete way that clearly separates it from everything else? We are certainly conditioned to consider it so. The movement of consciousness doesn't seem to sort the world into the form of bodies. The deeper fact of biology is symbiosis.

As we observe our thoughts, attention often shifts to the body. Then thought creates confusion by bringing in memories of aches, pain, and bodily feelings. How can we get out of this?

Getting out is not a problem. Use alcohol, drugs, religion, philosophy, complicated relationships, or any number of diversionary activities and you can get out. The more interesting question when we plunge into the world of body, pain, and suffering is, "What is it?"

This is the exploration of life in which we find ourselves. We can experiment. We know what a life of distraction is all about and we have presumably lost interest in that route. What other approach is there, as a question, and without a particular result wanted? What does diet do? Biofeedback? Exercise? Meditation? Homeopathy?

Ayurveda? Relationship? Dialogue? Silence? What is the phenomenon itself? What is the construction that occurs around the phenomenon? How is change restricted? Who am I if change is unrestricted?

By recognizing the mind as just the result of previous conditioning, I am free of feeling and thoughts. There is just space where this is taking place. How can love and compassion take place here?

How can love and compassion not take place here?

I keep having questions, but I never find satisfactory answers in which I can believe. How can I find answers to these questions?

This natural deconstruction of all the conclusions delivered to us by religion and philosophy is our intelligence, an inquiry that is not satisfied with belief. It is the question to life's answers. In part because of our conditioning and in part because of our biology, the certainty of conclusion appears to be the reason for our question. By questioning, we find an answer that spawns belief. If we can hold this system together, we have a kind of security. We believe we have the answers to our questions, so everything is fine. For some this works. For others, this does not.

The recognition of the constructed nature of belief systems leaves us with a different question altogether. This is the kind of question a young child who is not looking for an answer might have. The child is simply looking.

This is the nature of inquiry, an exploration into the nature of life, relationship, love, and spirituality as actuality, not as concept, belief, or ideation.

While the life of exploration is a very interesting life, it is also quite challenging, as the perception of life-as-it-is cuts through any collected belief. It is only dissatisfaction with our answers that compels us to look any further.

We each seem to hold back from a life of connectedness, using our beliefs as the reason. See what those beliefs are for you. Nothing really holds us back from contact with the actuality of life.

Awareness and the Nature of Thought

How can awareness operate in the midst of a terrifying situation, such as the threat of a heart attack?

The quality of awareness is not the assurance of bliss; rather, it is the contact with "as-isness." Sometimes terror is what is. We tend to try to change these qualities because of the basic aversion to them, without fully investigating them. Psychiatry, medical science, meditation, religious belief, and doing nothing are all possible avenues of investigation into the nature of these qualities. The denial of death is essential to the thought structure. The realization of the death of the self in each and every moment is the confrontation of our core illusion. When the body is involved, great care must be taken to eat modestly, exercise, and sleep adequately. Our bodies are hardly able to sustain the movement of consciousness, as they have organized so thoroughly around our thought structures. Great patience and care is in order. There is really nowhere to get in this. We have only actuality in which to reside.

If I stop trying to change or improve myself, what am I left with?

If we move outside of the perspective of changing the conditions of our mind, we are left with the question of what these conditions actually are. This can be discovered only in the space from which these conditions arise, not from the perspective that the conditions create. These mind states have a "goal," at the very base of which is survival.

We have to discover our own psychological death in order to fully discover what life is all about.

Can thought ever accept its own cessation? If thought can never accept the possibility of its cessation, how can we be peaceful with ourselves? Is it possible not only for the intellect, but the whole mind/body, to comprehend this very nature of continuous creation and cessation? Is there a concept of immortality instilled in us all through our conditioning that has become more real than the fact of cessation? How can we de-condition ourselves from this concept? Is this not why we are sad when a fellow mortal dies?

Thought can conceptualize itself, but does not appear to have the capacity to "see" itself in the sense of holistic comprehension or becoming conscious. However, it is not only possible but imminent in this very moment for the whole to comprehend the partial, for consciousness to see the mind. We do not need to de-condition ourselves from the sense of immortality, or denial of death, or fragmentation that thought produces. Rather, we can simply see the nature of mind, as it is, as an aspect of, but not actually different from, totality. Simply seeing thought in its inherent nature, without involving ourselves in its fragmentary perspective or trying to change it into something else, is the freedom we inherently possess.

The sorrow that is felt upon the death of another is both a deep connection to the human condition, compassion, and empathy, and at the same time the most fundamental of illusions that mankind carries. This paradox characterizes the human being, and is as it is.

Is the complete cessation of thought possible?

Psychological thought is constructed around the survival of the psychological "me." Functional thought is constructed around the actual survival of the bio-machine. The cessation we are interested in is not necessarily the non-arising of thought, or even the non-arising of psychological thought. Rather, let us consider non-involvement with psychological thought when it does arise and the intelligent engagement of functional thought when it occurs. It may be that through this non-involvement, the psychological thought tendency fades, but I would suggest that cessation is not anything but an unobtainable goal for most people.

Non-involvement is accessible for anyone, anywhere, without any special training, teacher, or method, simply by attending to thought. Simple attention, a non-doing in the most profound sense of the term, completely changes the appearance of psychological thought from substantial (as-if-real) to obviously mechanical. In the end, I am not concerned with the cessation of thought so much as seeing the "stickiness" of thought, which implies a doer. The doer can never be found.

I looked up "belief" in the dictionary. The definition was "mental acceptance of and conviction in the truth, actuality, or validity of something." What then would a life beyond belief be?

There has to be some kind of deconstruction of the educated or conditioned viewpoint, which believes substantially in its information. Part of this is coming to grips with the notion of self. Is it there, is it not, is it actual or imagined? This deconstruction has to take place without replacing the old ideas with a new set of ideas (non-dualism, Buddhism, fill-in-the-blankism).

Then perhaps the experimental construction of relationship, schools, communities, and other social institutions can take place. The common basis for this construction would be exploration, which is dynamic, rather than a fixed ideology.

The challenge might be that such an exploration, being fundamentally unstable, requires a deep stability in the individuals engaged in it. Ideologies don't require stability in the adherents since the ideology, being fixed, provides that.

Sometimes you talk about merging with the feeling, which implies giving attention to it. Let's say I experience a feeling of agitation. By "doing nothing," do you mean stop trying to change it and give your attention to it, or literally do absolutely nothing in relationship to that feeling?

I would suggest that you have already "given your attention to it." Otherwise you wouldn't apprehend the quality you are trying to change. Attention is a fact. This is transformative in itself. Trying to change something exerts a force from some other, imagined location and maintains a divided and conflicted world.

In exploring, I find that indeed thoughts and feelings arise spontaneously. They arise in awareness. The sense of me also arises in this awareness. My question is this: Am I this awareness? Or is it more accurate to say that this awareness is aware of me?

Does awareness exist outside of the thought of it? It might, but its attributes would not have "thing-ness," or reality, since they would not be thinkable. Much of what is taken as the nature of awareness—cultivating it, losing it—is in fact just the idea of what it might be. What if we approach from what it is not, and see what is left when that is set aside?

You suggest that this thought process—doing nothing, doing something —is the problem itself. How to get out of this conundrum? Just observe the tension of this doing no-thing and doing some-thing? We want to spring into action, do we not?

The creator of the conundrum now wants to spring into action, but will the action release us, or make our situation more complicated? Thought insists that something needs to be fixed, but what needs to be fixed when thought falls silent and our hearts envelop the other in our self? Being, not doing, is the expression of this realization.

Thought, as technology, allows us to function out of being, but can never be useful in the discovery of being itself.

I would like to know more about what you mean by "dialogue."

For me, dialogue is the simple recognition that our life is porous, with no inner or outer, and for that matter, no awareness or unawareness. There is no place to stand to define a "me" and a "you." What seems to remain in that recognition is dialogue, the movement of life. This is only a description. Your life is the actuality, and perhaps you already have noted its dialogic nature.

A few years ago I learned I could no longer lie about things. It was amazing how quickly family and friends dropped away from me. I did nothing in particular to offend; I merely stopped pretending. Now I am in that position you describe so clearly: I am alone. I have the feeling I will never have another friend. It is a constant struggle for me to stay alert to the trap of the mind. Although the process is direct and simple, there also seems to be something artificial about it.

You have obviously understood a great deal about the illusion of the conceptual world, and the ideas and dishonesties that people use to structure their so-called relationships to each other. But has this understanding become fixed? You have placed yourself under the burden of your own understanding, and as you have pointed out, in some ways this is worse than the oblivion out of which your understanding grew. Struggling to stay alert to the trap of the mind is the trap of the mind.

Discard your understanding, discard the moment, and discard the pressure of maintaining anything in particular. The fact of life is presenting itself to each of us without our effort, and the fact is that we are in relationship with or without our effort or our understanding. This dialogue is the expression of our relatedness. The possibilities of any relationship are limited only by our ideas. This is the challenge we each have—how to embody the expression of our heart, to live it fully in our life.

Emptiness

You describe the concept of emptiness. Can you describe how it manifests itself? Can you give the definition of emptiness?

Emptiness defies definition. It's the absence of; it's not the presence of. So if it's the absence of everything, it's also the absence of definition.

Does emptiness include the angry bosses and crying babies in our lives?

In what way are they in our lives? If I have an angry boss, I have to be an unhappy employee. The angry boss is there only if I am somebody in relation to that boss. If I'm nobody in relation to that angry boss, the angry boss doesn't exist. If I walk into your workplace, and your boss is angry at you, I don't experience the same thing because I don't have a role in that. Your baby crying doesn't affect me the same way as my baby crying, because I don't have the identity. So if emptiness is the absence of identity, it's also the absence of the difficulty that comes with identity. It's not the absence of life. Life is still going on, but that's the undiscovered life.

So then the emptiness can be described as the absence of a "me" that's involved at the ego level?

It could be, but that would be filling the emptiness with some idea.

If I have an angry boss and I want to relate intelligently to him, why is being in a state of emptiness advantageous?

There's no advantage. The word "advantage" suggests a position in a strategy. An angry boss cannot be angry in an empty space. The boss has to be angry about something, presumably about you, the employee. You have to take that role to experience that anger.

And if I'm detached from that role, then I can respond intelligently to it, and it won't be a catastrophe.

It's not a formula like that. If you're detached from that role, you probably won't be in that role. The fact is, you're attached to that role. You think you're an employee. You think that you're being subjected to an angry boss, so you're in a lot of difficulty. That's where you are.

I do work there, so I identify myself as an employee.

Turn it into a question. Why do I work here? What am I doing here? That question will shatter the framework in which you exist in relation to an angry boss. You work there. Why? Because you enjoy the work, you hate the work, you're making money. Why are you making money? To pay the mortgage. Why are you paying the mortgage? To have the house. Why do you have the house? It goes on and on. If you follow that question through your whole life, you may not need to be in relation to an angry boss.

So in that emptiness we don't identify with who we think we are. We are able to be objective.

You're creating the idea of being unidentified, and now emptiness is an ideal. The fact of our life is that we are identified. Emptiness is something that we don't know anything about. Now from the identified state we say we want to know about emptiness, but the identified state cannot know about emptiness, it can know only about where it actually is. You don't need to create an alternative to your life. Consider what you are living—the actuality of where you are—and see its true nature.

A cartoon someone sent me once might be helpful here.

Emerging from the cave of the recluse, the quirky fellow looks out over the valley below. The caption: "Nothing in his experience had prepared him for nothing in his experience."

Do you believe in some form of intelligence behind the evolution of life and the existence of the universe?

I don't believe in belief. If you want to take on a belief system, then you could take on, for example, the Christian Creationist belief. You would have to make a jump of faith at the point of creation, which is to say, you have to go from "I don't know" to "I believe." Likewise, if you go into the scientific paradigm, you have to make a similar leap: "I don't know how the universe began, but I believe that there was a big bang." There is no difference between "God created the universe" and "the Big Bang created the universe." In both cases you have to make that leap from "I don't know," which is authentic and actual, to "I believe."

So belief is not rooted in the authentic and actual?

Belief is rooted in the discomfort with not knowing. Explore that state of "I don't know" and see what that is, rather than short-circuit that by overlaying an idea of any sort.

No matter how noble?

The thing about noble ideas is that they're noble in a certain context. It was very noble for the Crusaders to head off to Jerusalem to conquer the Muslims. Except if you were a Muslim. Then it wasn't noble. If you were a Muslim, it was noble to fight the Crusaders.

You note that we are living in a fragmented world. Do you see any hope for the human race or will we eventually destroy ourselves?

Hope isn't particularly necessary. Hope is a projection of some different state than what we're in now. I think it would be much more useful to understand where we are than to speculate on whether or not there's some other place that we could be. The qualities that are expressed right now in the human condition are clearly painful and destructive. Whether we have the capacity for any other kind of expression —for love—requires that each of us understand where we actually are. Let's begin here and now.

Isn't the concept of "doing nothing" misleading if it implies doing something other than what you are doing now? Isn't trying to do nothing useless?

All concepts are misleading in that they are symbols. Concepts have no inherent "thing-ness," but only appear to have substance outside of the thought itself. The way I am using "doing nothing" is to describe the futility in the attempt of the conceptual "me" to change itself. "Me" is a thought, and is insubstantial outside of the thought itself. It has no means to see itself, change itself, get better, or get worse. Trying to do nothing, trying to change—all this trying business is thinking. Thought doesn't have anything else to do but to think. Just because something is pointless doesn't mean we won't occupy our lives thinking it or "doing it."

You seem to be talking from your own non-dual experience at times, without calling it such. Yet you also talk about contrasts—consciousness as limitless, and thought as restricted, which seems to be a dualistic point of view.

I don't know anything about non-duality. I wouldn't call myself anything in particular, or for that matter, a non-anything. We really don't know much other than that we have suddenly become aware, and we are investigating this strange and wonderful world we have landed in. I have no idea where we are, what we are, or even *if* we are. All the available spiritual maps appear to be outdated. Belief systems require our blindness, and we have become aware of that, so we can no longer believe. Thought is symbolic; it is not the thing it represents. Teachers offer us the security of surety for the small price of our integrity. All we are left with is to explore. This is not an exploration of doing, but of being.

No Place to Stand

One of the most intriguing ideas in your work is how thought itself creates the idea of a thinker. Could you talk more about that?

That's interesting, isn't it? There isn't simply a thought stream and the attendant awareness of that stream. There also arises the sense of a thinker who is thinking the thoughts. It's the creation of a subject-object universe. And that's a very special feature, which is particularly delusional. The thought stream itself, in its simplest form, is just a functional readout of the environment. As such, this is a very fine thing because we need to know about the environment.

But this creation of the thinker or the "me"—the world of the thinker, the specialness of the thinker, the power of the thinker—is a very interesting process. This is where a split takes place in human consciousness between a factual mechanical thought, which serves to organize and predict the environment, and a psychological sense of self—not a biological or factual self, but a psychological self. The creation of that sense of self by thought is responsible for all the cultural, social, and relational structures that are currently working so poorly.

Can you consider, for example, a thought stream that had as its organizing "macro-thought" a communal sensibility? We would then think in terms of the family, or village, or country, or human race, much like an ant or a honeybee. They have a form of thinking going on, but it's really a communal thinking. I'm not suggesting that we should aspire to become some kind of worker bee, just that there are any number of ways that thought could have been organized.

It's interesting that thought organizes itself the way it does in individuals and societies. It is also clear that it's not working very well. When we become collectively aware of this fact, and when we start to investigate it through quantum physics or philosophy or experience, we begin to see that the world as we know it is an idea.

So has consciousness made a mistake?

I don't think consciousness is an actor in that way. There is no such thing as a mistake, because consciousness is everything. Besides, I really wouldn't want to speak for consciousness. I'll let consciousness speak for itself.

I would recommend that each of us see what consciousness is doing in relation to this question of a subject-object world and the sense of self and the thought stream. Let consciousness speak, because consciousness *is* speaking. It is immanent. We are all in contact with it.

Thankfully I don't have to speak for consciousness. I just have to speak for the aberration of the thought world, with which I am very familiar, as we all are. That's the wonderful thing about life. The depth and the expansion of life are held not by a few, but by each of us.

Is awareness evolving or is it us? Maybe awareness is the changing, constant flow of things.

I would have to stand in one place in relationship to the rest of life in order to answer that question (and a rather good question it is). I can't find a place to stand. I'll keep you informed of any progress in this regard.

I can understand the necessity and usefulness of a model of consciousness to prompt the scientific community to seriously inquire into the nature of consciousness. But what use, if any, do such models have for the individual?

One value may be to make transparent the assumptions that we are currently operating under, and how we construct our collective reality. There are implicit models already imbedded in our conceptualization.

Any model is an attempt to understand or predict the attributes of what is being modeled. This allows the technologist to manipulate that which is modeled. Consciousness has eluded this technology, and what is generally passed off as a model of consciousness is typically mind-thinking-of-consciousness in very elaborate, grandiose, or beautiful ways such as religion and philosophy.

I think time, space, and ego are false. I think birth and death are both part of life—eternal life—in which we are all living. I don't understand this great mystery but it sure is fun.

If there is something that is whole, and the expression of the eternal, then it must touch each of us, regardless of our background, and with or without our efforts to find it. Perhaps this is the cutting edge of human consciousness, the rudimentary beginnings of our collective capacity to directly experience unindividuated consciousness.

Lately I have been experiencing lucid dreaming, in which the dream world becomes very vivid, and there is the clear understanding that dreaming is happening while I'm in the dream. I also have the sense that I have fallen out of timelessness and into separation when I awaken. What do you make of this?

It's never clear to me that I have fallen out of, rather than through, or into, something. Or more simply, without looking back to this thing we have fallen from, would we not be in something that is without reference, without obvious framework? It seems that the qualities change—the intensity, the sense of location, etc.—but the referencing and comparison is what seems to create conflict. If there is only one thing happening, and that one thing is the sense of separation in time, then is it the same or different from the timeless quality that seems to have passed?

Many dreams are without significance and are the result of too much input during the day, spicy or heavy foods too late in the day, or other such influences. Another kind of dream is prophetic (indicates what is coming) or synthetic (integrates what has happened) and is often unnoticed, since it is mind talking to itself in symbols. Yet another kind is not personal, but deals with archetypal forces, or broad psychic energies—for example, the play of good and evil. Perhaps there is another kind that is transformative, in which consciousness or formlessness moves through the world of form and fundamentally alters the condition of that form.

I would say that some dreams have significance and these dreams are apparent as such, but most dreams are the result of too much salsa or TV. Simplifying one's diet and activity leads to a quieter and more vivid dream state.

There appear to be two schools of thought. One is like Krishnamurti's, which implies free will for breaking through, and the other is like Balsekar's, which says there is no free will, and that all is pre-determined, even the desire to break through. Somehow, my instinct tells me that life is like an improvisation rather than a fixed script. While I once had a powerful experience of being lived by life, it still felt like an improvisation, a potential, rather than a fixed plan. This also accords with quantum physics. What do you think?

Thought always appears to have a choice. Thought's essential function is to measure and predict, to present the best possibilities for our survival. In this respect, we live in a world of choosing. But this choosing, this free will, has a mechanical quality to it, and while it may appear to be free, it is free only to roam the confines of its conceptual interpretation.

Consciousness appears unconcerned with the choices that thought is so caught up in. Consciousness attends to the choosing of the conceptual world. It simply is. It is choiceless. Yet while this unmoving beingness may appear to be uninvolved, it has a tremendously dynamic, transformative quality to it. It changes everything it touches.

But this is not the end of the story, because there is no thought separate from consciousness, in actuality. There is only one, and this singularity, the collapse of the two into one, the merger of consciousness and thought, has the qualities of both aspects. Life itself, whole and undivided, is the doer, the action, and the result of the action, neither predestined nor possessing free will. The wholeness of life holds the potential of infinite possibilities in the timelessness of each moment, and yet in the expression of each moment there is only one thing happening. Upon this one thing happening, there is only one thing that could have happened.

Since we tend to think in either/or terms, this both/and quality of life is most elegantly expressed by the poet, the quantum physicist, and the mystic. It is the great experiment of life—the great improvisation as you put it—to discover what occurs when consciousness and thought are not held as separate.

Transformation

Some of us have had the paradigm-shifting experience of being more than the ego or the body, either through drugs or meditation. And since that experience, we have tried to bring together those aspects of being—the self and that which is beyond the self. Can you offer some insight into that attempt?

We have typically approached the absolute from the relative, trying to draw in the absolute. Conceptual spirituality is about the interpretation of silence through words. Rather than trying to grab the absolute from the point of view of our ideas, let the absolute infuse the relative.

Can we access the absolute by simply allowing things to happen, rather than by shaping our lives in a certain way?

Life is moving through us. The quality of undivided energy or consciousness is moving through the relative qualities of our mind and body. But the distortion of thought, which by its nature always divides and wants to have control, makes us think we're going to grab that energy and use it, because we know what to do with it. We're going to use it to save the world, or overpower someone, or give lectures about the absolute. But we don't need to grab it; it's grabbing us.

So in some way we should sit with it and not try to fix anything, including ourselves.

Regardless of what we're trying to do to fix ourselves psychologically, the effort is wasted. The quality that we're talking about, which is no-mind, does not require effort. It infuses everything already. It's the very sub-stratum of our world.

So how do you reach it? We are so busy. We think, "I gotta do this, gotta have that, gotta get money, gotta have a relationship."

How do you open a closed fist so it can receive? There's nothing you can do to relax the fist. It simply relaxes and opens. There isn't an action you can take. This is the difficulty of the mind. The mind searches for the exit within its own structure. It looks for silence within the field of thought. But there's no silence within the field of thought—there's only more thought. There's big thought, bigger thought, really big thought, God thought, but it's still just thought. And thought, looking for silence in itself, can never find it.

Perhaps because of my humanity, I find I have a great desire to describe the ineffable. I feel that I'm going to go on wondering what that is and what we're all about.

The mind is curious. That's not going to stop. My mind is not different from your mind. All the attributes that you can describe about your mind, I can discover in mine. But I don't have any feeling that my curiosity is ever going to find a resolution. There is irritation that typically comes with needing to find the answer right now. The mind is structured to do that. But we can find the question, rather than the answer. The real question, not the curiosity question, is in the ground of silence. When that question contacts everything, it changes it. It's like our whole world is turned backwards, in a mirror image. The world of mind seems to be what we are. But in fact it's the world of silence that we are, and mind is just where it plays out.

You talk about the difference between faith and belief, the ability to live a life of faith that is free of belief. I think most people see those concepts as synonymous. But there's a tremendous feeling of faith in life expressing itself through all of us. What you're saying is that we can trust that life force.

We really don't need to run the show. The show is being run through us and through every other living thing. That's a very faith-based perspective, and it relieves us of the burden of having to believe. The problem with belief is that it requires us to have a particular set of ideas that is different from all other sets of ideas. It is the creation of distinction that generates belief. It also generates conflict. It is the basis of war, of separation, of all the human horrors that we've seen throughout history. Faith, on the other hand, is the discarding of those beliefs. It is the possibility of peace, health, community, understanding—all those things that we aspire to through our beliefs.

Belief is, in some way, a bastardization or distortion of this fundamental intelligence that we all experience. But when the intelligence started to stir in us, we went to somebody and asked, "What is this?" They answered, "Believe in this set of ideas," because they didn't really know what it was either. What they might have said is, "Actually, I don't know what it is, but it's moving in me too so maybe we should sit down together and explore it."

We must deconstruct our belief systems in order to return again to that primal awareness of life or feeling of God's spirit flowing through us.

In the "doing" realm of spirituality, all you can really do is deconstruct your intellectual collections. You can't do anything positively about the intelligence of life, although that intelligence may be able to do a lot of things about you.

So nothing is required positively. We can deconstruct. It's the negative approach, the *via negativa.* Every time we cling to a positive idea, we're simply plastering that idea over the top of reality. Reality doesn't require any ideas. It already has everything—all ideas, all concepts. It is everything. Reality needs absolutely nothing.

The first time I came upon the word "deconstruct" in your work, I was immediately put in mind of the post-modern viewpoint that when we deconstruct meaning we will find that there's really nothing left. All of what we take to be reality is a construct, a matter of personal belief and perception. But what you're saying is that when we deconstruct meaning, what we are left with is vibrant "life-as-it-is."

That's the difference between having an intellectual philosophy about deconstruction and actually doing it in your life. When you actually strip away your entire collection of concepts, you aren't left with "nothing." You're left with everything. You're left with life itself. There is something vital that is energetically moving through our systems. You can't strip that away, because it is the totality of everything.

So it's not a philosophical stance, it is a living stance. It is a fact we can each come to in our lives through direct exploration. It is an invitation to everyone else to find out for himself. No one should accept anything we are talking about without that exploration. Otherwise, it will just become another philosophy, and I'm not interested in creating the next philosophy.

There's nothing you can do to prepare. If you can do nothing, then, in fact, you've prepared. Can you completely disengage the idea of getting somewhere without that becoming a new somewhere to get to, and without taking that language and making a new system out of it?

Some people seem to be suffering more than others. There's some sort of resistance happening on their part.

Sometimes suffering is the process of change in a life, and the resistance to it is the sense of difficulty. But there are a lot of people who say they are happy when it appears that they're actually suffering. When you're at the dentist, and you've got the pain killer, and they're drilling your tooth, is there pain even if you can't feel it? Would you want to feel the pain and know that there's damage happening to your tooth? Is psychological suffering the full contact with the movement of your life, or is it actually something bad that we should relieve?

You had the insight that you were chasing power. And then, when you had that insight you stopped doing that.

No, I wouldn't say that! I wish that were true. That would make a really good story: I had some meeting, some experience, some event, and at that moment power dropped away and I became a far better person. No, the whole construct of power, escape from death, and control over the world, is created each time thought arises. That's the very nature of thought. Thought takes the universe, which is whole, and divides it into two or more things. And then thought begins to model how we are going to survive, how we can move without getting destroyed. That very arising of thought is the arising of fear, of division, and the drive for power.

Why does the spiritual search end up being about power?

Spirituality is a fear-based construction. While we like to think of it as a more positive thing, people are terrified. We're afraid of death and we want to have a confirmed story that it's not the case, that we go on, that there's something more. One of the ways through that is to convince yourself you have the power to change it. When you get into very, very subtle areas of mind, you can begin to see how you can literally construct reality. You can alter the nature of the way things are. And that starts to look very close to being able to escape death, because if I can move reality, then I can move death.

Sustained Transcendence

I'd like to make a distinction between people who have had a taste of the transcendent experience and people who are in the taste, who don't necessarily fluctuate in and out of it, but who have the sustained transcendent experience. What is your perception of this?

The general notion of the sustained transcendent experience is a construction. For example, I could have a brain tumor and have what appears to be sustained transcendence, and later it is obvious that there is a brain tumor. Now, did the transcendence create the tumor? Was the vehicle, the physical body, unable to handle the movement of that energy? Or did the tumor create the change and the perception? Are we talking about abnormal brain chemistry? Abnormal brain structure? Or something that is other than the physicality of the brain? We're really talking about a construction that we're agreeing upon, which is that there is something called transcendent experience that is other than life experience. This construction can be deconstructed, leaving us simply with the as-is-ness of life.

What I would call the sustained transcendent experience would be the collapse of the construction of all our experience into the actuality of life. In that respect, you and I, and all God's children, are the same. We're all in it, and of it, and we'll always be in and of it. All the time. The only difference would be whether you and I construct a story around that. And if you construct the story that you're not in it, and of it, but you're outside of it trying to get to it, then your world will be that. And if I construct the story that I'm beyond it, then that's going to be my story. If I can convince you I'm beyond it and you're not in it, then you're going to come to me as a student, and I'll be your teacher.

Perceiving this, you're left with a deconstructed state where you can't produce a new story. That is the fundamental disbelief in belief, a fundamental perception of the way that we create reality.

Would you say that you have experienced a loss of self?

Where is the so-called self located? I have searched long and hard for a self and haven't found it anywhere. It appears to not be lost, but rather to never have been there to begin with. The concept of self occurs as part of every thought. This continues to occur when thought does, but isn't this obvious as thought? There is the collapse into a unitary world where only one thing is happening. It would seem that we all share this attribute, but the nature of thought (which projects multiplicity) often veils the obvious fact of oneness.

So you have integrated the self with the non-self?

I have no sense of a self with a non-self, or of seeing anything that was hidden, or any transition from something to something else. How would I know if such occurred? This is not to say that such did not occur, simply that there is no possible knowing of this occurring.

Did you experience an event of bliss?

No event. I've had bliss. Well, I think I had bliss…at least once. At least I have the memory of having bliss. Does this count?

Have you experienced sustained transcendence?

Experience as a description of life is very limited. The function of thought is to capture what has occurred and to try to predict the future through that modality. As a technology of survival, experience is very useful. But the experience of the expansion of self into God and the dissolution of the identity—that experience becomes a description that I am driven to either sustain or to reproduce. That is perhaps the subtlest trap of the mind. So many people are looking for the experience they had decades ago in Nepal when they dropped acid and saw God. The rest of their life is spent looking for that experience. The very nature of the "experience" that we're talking about is that it's outside of experience. It's outside of mind. It can't be captured by a mechanical process. It can't be reproduced.

Is your perception related to a particular event?

No.

It evolved through time?

No.

It always was?

No. What we're talking about is outside of time. And being outside of time, it is outside of that whole historic context. Transcendent experience, or non-experience, is outside of any of the events that you can catalog in your life, outside of the center, the self, the ideas. It's not in any of that, so you can't locate it anywhere.

If you read carefully, in some of the descriptions of "transcendent experience" you'll find this is implied or actually stated outright. When the individual says, "I met this person and this happened, and when I dropped into the transcendent state I dropped out of that whole context." Well, why do you need to bring the context into it if we're not in that context? The whole point is that the context that we're creating is the illusion. What would be the point of answering your question in this way: "In India, I walked into a little village and the holy man tapped me on the head. Then I dropped out of that whole context and discovered the quality that had always been there and would always be"? If it always has been, then there's no particular point.

You have said that there is a very fine line between the mystic and the madman.

I consider myself to be both. It's the same thing, really, because in both cases you understand that reality is simply an agreed-upon construction. In the case of the mystic, there's the capacity to communicate that. In the madman, the capacity to communicate has broken down through some kind of separation. That's the only difference.

Could you tell if someone else is in a mystic or madman state?

Generally the only thing you know about another person is what you project. If you're not projecting, then you are the other person, and you have direct contact. But you're also all people at that point. So I think the very idea that there's this discreet location that has a different state from the other discreet locations around it, is a structural error. Because it's not really the way life is. Life isn't located in me, separate from you. If I've structured it in that way through my concepts, then when I meet you, I meet only my ideas of you. If I say, "Oh yes, she has the 52 attributes of enlightenment," that's because I read a book on how to tell that. So yes, you're enlightened by my criteria.

Life is simply bubbling up in these wave-like forms and then crashing back into itself. If that's enlightenment, great. But I don't think the ocean of life considers itself enlightened. It's just the ocean of life.

Many seekers are aspiring toward having such an experience. Can someone prepare for a sustained transcendent experience?

No. The preparation comes through taking on a belief system, and the practice always has with it an end result. If I sit on my cushion, I will experience the list of things described in the literature, by the teacher, by the system, by the philosophy. We experience those things as we were promised, simply because we construct them. If we have difficulty constructing them, then we sit on a cushion for a long time before we construct the experience we're supposed to have.

How could you possibly prepare for something that is not constructed by thought? What would that preparation be?

The Other Side

THE OTHER SIDE

The seeker, in his searching, comes to the river. Across the river a yogi is in deep contemplation. The seeker calls out to him, "Can you help me get to the other side?"

The yogi looks up from his meditation and replies, "You're on the other side."

As long as we believe that we will find something to fill our emptiness and quench our pain, explain the paradox of life and assuage its vagaries, give us substance and meaning, we will fill our days with the quixotic spiritual search. This relationship to life may have the trappings of the spiritual, but it is essentially self-centered. It is not a search for the dissolution of self or even the integration of self, but the expression of narcissism in its most duplicitous form.

Religious, philosophical, and spiritual systems suggest that we must go through some process, some systematic search, some basic preparation. But they are all built upon a false premise: that we must do something to discover the timeless now. There is no lack of access to the immediate moment. No preparation is needed to be where we are—in that present. In the immediate there is no "me" to be found.

The self is constructed out of thoughts strung like beads on the string of time—a sense of past and future, memory, and anticipation. But thought, time, and self are entirely conceptual. We search for resolution within a conceptual world in which there is no actual resolution. There are just the concepts of searching and searcher, and the concept that the searcher finds meaning and purpose through searching.

This search is in vain. The searcher, which is the core sense of self, is both the problem we seek to solve and the problem that searches for the solution. This fundamental realization brings the spiritual life as we know it to a screeching halt. It is over. There is nothing to do because there is no doer. There is nothing to resolve, nothing to fill, nothing to fix.

But this is not the end; it is the beginning. Coming to the end of the spiritual search is the end of spirituality and the beginning of spirit-actuality. Spirit-actuality is not the expression of our need for something, the search for something, or the absence of something. It is the expression of the actuality of spirit, the articulation of what life brings to us, the exploration of unity, in which we are at once a part and the whole. The perspective has changed from the "me" looking for resolution to a "me" turned inside out and upside down—"we"-consciousness peering through the eyes of "me."

This perspective is complete, so the game has changed. The point is not to find but to look. Like an adult playing hide-and-seek with a young child, the integral perspective is fully aware of the position of the ego and the deficiency of its hiding place. Finding and exposing the self is not the challenge. It is found and exposed every moment as thought arises and passes away. The fragility of its posturing is obvious to the most casual of our glances.

Don't we know that the self is a concoction? Don't we know where it hides? We know that we cannot base the expression of our life on this infantile creation of thought. Life must be based on something more substantial, grounded, and connected than the conceptual self. From this basis, perhaps, the structures of thought can grow up into a yet unseen maturity.

The radical abandonment of spirituality in its entirety is the first step of a life of inquiry freed from the demands of attainment, an exploration not restricted to the archaic notion of enlightenment. The end of spirituality is the recognition of an integral perspective as the fact in which we are all at play.

The expression of our life then becomes not the search for this awareness, the self looking for its cessation, the "me" looking for something more or better. Rather, the expression of our life becomes that of consciousness itself, which is, by its nature, inclusive and connected.

The Tale of the Spiritual Journey

You talk about ending the spiritual search. Should we stop searching?

The whole concept of spirituality is a contrivance. It posits that there is a spiritual world and a non-spiritual world. What's the non-spiritual world? If I wake up and go to work in the morning, is that non-spiritual? If you take away the conceptualization of spirituality, then isn't everything spiritual? Then what are spiritual practices for? Why are we trying to get to this spiritual world if we are already in the midst of it? There's nothing wrong with spirituality, other than that it doesn't actually exist.

Could you talk about the process that caused you to see things as you do?

My so-called process is really irrelevant, just as is yours. Do you want to talk about it on that basis? We've all come on a journey of some sort, through difficulty, challenge, and the attempt to find resolution of conflict by engaging in politics, religion, spirituality, or psychology. At some point, perhaps, we realize that the accumulation of information isn't helpful. It's just more experience crammed into our brain on top of everything else that was already there.

Generally when we look back on our life, we do so with judgment, to make a conclusion. Otherwise, what is there to look back on? When I look back on my life without judgment or conclusion, I'm like an infant looking at phenomena without the organizing principal of language. That is to say, I can't understand what happened.

It's only when I organize my life in a verbal way that it makes sense. For example, I could organize it around spiritual events: important teachers, great transmissions, openings, experiences, visions of God, dark nights of the soul.

What about just seeing your conditioning? I look back on my life and I see how the conditioning affects the present moment.

But I see conditioning only because I learned there was something called conditioning. If I were a professor speaking to my colleagues, I would look back on my life in terms of my academic achievements. If I were a man at a bar, trying to pick up a woman, I would be thinking of accomplishments that society would recognize: money, power, my car (shiny, bright, parked outside, hopefully a sports car). We can look at our life only from a perspective. The perspective is: what events in that life do I judge to be good or bad? If I look without the judgment, what am I looking at?

I look at my life in terms of seeing what I can really let go of. It helps me see illusion and conditioning.

But isn't the fundamental conditioning that of referring back to the past? Why do this? We look back so we can determine what to do next.

Maybe we can reach a point where we don't have to look back. But first, perhaps, we must look back to learn about ourselves.

What do we find in referring to the past?

Sometimes it helps me see that I live in the illusion of thought, conditioned by things that I decided in my childhood. I made decisions for the sake of survival, and I don't really have to live by those decisions anymore. I may be holding on to something that isn't helping me survive; I just thought it was. If I didn't refer back, I don't think I would see this.

And what if you didn't see that? Would the thing that you see when you refer back exist? What if from this point forward you don't look back?

There is just the memory. But that memory is just an object like anything else.

The bundle of ideas I have about the memory interprets the memory.

It's also conceivable to look at a memory without interpretation, as I look at this vase of flowers without interpretation.

Yes, and then what is it? If you look at the flowers and they're not flowers, because there is no name or interpretation, what are they?

I don't know, but that's what they are.

When I look back without the judger, what happened is completely baffling. It looks like chaos. It cannot be organized in any intelligent way.

But you also recognize that you can't say if it was a waste of time or not from that vantage point.

That's right. I really have nothing to say about it, because I don't know what it was or how it informs anything about where I am right now. Neither is helpful in describing the biographical journey that we all would like to have in our life.

But maybe also at some practical level, you can see that the movement of life uses whatever you came from.

Whatever that accumulation is, it is being expressed, or "used," as you say.

Given this understanding of history and its interpretation, can you tell me anything about your spiritual search before you stopped?

First, let's understand that whatever my so-called search was, it was useless. The very premise of looking—the premise that something was missing, something was wrong with me—was mistaken, so the search was irrelevant. The story of my search is like any other story. It is fiction. I can tell you about the great teachers I met, the terrible austerities I underwent, the months and years of meditation I spent relentlessly looking for truth. That would be fiction.

I could tell you the story of a young man who was like many of the post-World War generation. He grew up in a country racked by political turmoil, social injustice, politics by assassination, and leadership by hypocrisy. This was the United States in the sixties and seventies. This young man was involved in politics like many of his generation, until he saw that politics could never solve the problem of the human condition.

The young man saw so many friends fall along the way, those who gave up, gave in, sold out, or succumbed to the world of mental illness or drug and alcohol addiction. In this chaos, the world of spirituality had a powerful appeal, with its teachers of surety, the workers of wonders and givers of grace. And that is what it turned out to be—the appeal of power. In the face of confusion, so many of us chose authority, magical thinking, and belief. We were not searching for truth or for love; we were looking for power and control, for safety. We were infants looking for father and mother.

It is easy to see that the search of the young man in that world of teachers of spirit, of magicians and miracle workers, of yogis and lamas, is a fiction. The story collapsed under the weight of its own fantastic need for a happy ending in which the seeker merges with the universe, but is still there to tell all his friends about it.

There was never a search, only the attempt to acquire power and control over life. This idea, based on the notion of separation, is unrelated to any actuality. As such, there is no obvious beginning or end, no point of resolution. Accounts of sudden shifts are interesting in that they imply a before and after, a kind of dualism maintained as memory in the after phase. If there is no before or after, no time to sequence events, then when is the end of the search or the beginning of the search? For that matter, what is the search and who is searching?

So, when you ask about my search, you are asking me to tell a story.

You say enlightenment is a myth, but how did you arrive at your understanding, if not through experiences?

If I describe a series of experiences that came to a certain point, after which I was different, don't we really have a restatement of the enlightenment game? Then whatever I describe as what I did to get to that point will be what the listener will want to do. When I look at the question—"Have I transformed, have I changed from something before to something after?"—I don't find any point of change. There has always been this ground of awareness, which has always been accessible. There have always been thoughts arising and passing away in that ground. The shift of perspective that moves the field of awareness to the foreground and thoughts to the background has always been there.

Whatever story I tell is fiction. I pursued whatever approaches to understanding I could find, including long periods of meditation, particularly in Asia. I had contact with some very obscure but powerful teachers. And I found that the discovery I sought was not in all those pursuits. At the end of all that, I discovered that I was still there. All the qualities that I started with were still there. Now that's a very interesting thing. What I discovered was that I'm a human being. That was the point of connection—my humanness, not some state I created to get away from it.

What would you say a human being is?

That's what we all are; it's inescapable. We can try to escape by creating perfection or some alternative quality that is not conflicted or painful, but in the end that's an attempt to run away from something, not an attempt to make contact with something.

What took place in your searching that allowed you to realize that there was no longer anything to search for?

You are still asking about a point of transformation. You are positing a period of life before this point, which is in one state of mind. There is the point of transformation, and then there is the rest of the life, which is lived in a fundamentally different way. This is the enlightenment myth. For me to indicate a point at which I realized enlightenment was a myth, and that there was no need for a spiritual search, would just be another version of the enlightenment fiction. This would just reinforce the lunacy we seem to be caught up in.

I don't see a difference in my being now, before, or ever. It seems to me that whatever it is that is here, has always been here. There is no causal relationship that I can find between any of the spiritual practices I have undergone and the state of being in which we all exist. Whether you meditate or not, do yoga or not, have a guru or not, the access point to all of reality is always in reach, always available, always here in this moment.

What religion was practiced in your home when you were growing up, and were you influenced by it?

I was raised in a Quaker household. Quakers have very little ritual in their belief system, but they have a great love for Jews and Catholics. If you go to Quaker retreat centers you'll always find priests, nuns, and rabbis. Maybe the Quakers are attracted to the ritual, and practitioners of the ritualistic religions in turn are looking for the simplicity of the Quakers.

When I was a child I was exposed to the works of Martin Buber and Thomas Merton. There was a steady stream of politicos, mendicant visionaries, fringe mystics, and alternative thinkers flowing through the Quaker meeting house. The Quakers are interesting people, very nice people, who are generally trying hard to be kind and loving. I could sit quietly in a Quaker meeting even as a child, but I wasn't a Quaker. I wasn't a Quaker because I wasn't a Christian. Trying to be loving wasn't the same as finding the root of my fear, and even though Quakerism was founded by an ecstatic mystic, I found neither ecstasy nor mysticism in Quakerism.

Do you align yourself with any teachers or traditions?

Early on, I was a consumer of a wide array of spiritual teachers. I found that my focus was never on the spiritual philosophy I was studying, but on the transformative powers of the teacher I was encountering. Could this individual actually change me? Could this individual give me experiences beyond what I already knew? Could grace or shakti be imparted?

So, I was an impatient, arrogant, and demanding student, but I did find that most of the teachers were teachers of information, not of transformation. When I found the few who were transformers, I felt I had hit pay dirt. These people were able to shift the energy of my psychic field, give me experiences, and show me what seemed to be a boundless universal unity.

But the transformers—these powerful teachers—either went power-mad, got caught up with sex scandals or money scandals, or otherwise imploded. I had a few encounters with individuals who seemed tremendously powerful, but they were, strangely enough, either anonymous or barely public in their expression. They had no interest in manifesting the power that seemed to me to reside in them. They seemed amused at my drive for this spiritual power, my impatience, and my demands for demonstration of their spiritual prowess. What they threw back to me was, "What are you afraid of?" Well, what was I afraid of?

This was a whole different matter, indeed. The spiritual quest, the noble search, the expression of everything that is good, was suddenly reduced to a neurotic expression of my own fear. I wasn't on a spiritual search; fear was on a spiritual search. This "me" is fear. What could fear possibly find other than more of its own kind? And, let's face it, there is no purer expression of fear than power.

The great teacher-transformers suddenly seemed like terrified children. The spiritual search was a sham. Without the sham, the world is just as it is. Everything is spiritual and nothing is spiritual. So, no, I don't align myself with a teacher or tradition.

Coming to the end of the spiritual search is coming to this realization that everything and nothing is spiritual?

It isn't a realization. It is the exhaustion of the idea of spirituality. This idea creates the division of the spiritual and the non-spiritual.

You have no idea how the discovery occurred? I find it interesting that you feel that the "how" of the discovery is not relevant, or is meaningless. If it was always known anyway, why was there a time in your life when you felt like you were seeking and doing?

Language is difficult here. The narrative comes from the conceptual. But from the "perspective" of the One, nothing has done anything in particular—since there is no causality, separation, location, or time. Rather, in beingness there is simply "as-isness." How can we talk about a point of change, discovery, enlightenment, or merger, since that places us outside of this beingness, and gives us a before and after, a location, and a process?

Many examples in life could lead one to believe that both realities are true. It depends on what perspective you want to take. If you are the searcher, you search. If you are It, then there is only One. There is no search, searcher, or searched.

If we were not human, there would be no search. There would be no discovery. Is not the purpose of our human life to discover Oneness and become more like It?

This is certainly how it appears, but I would suggest that you have it backwards.

Life is not about the discovery of Oneness by the relative, but rather the expression of Oneness in the relative. Since we are conditioned to have the vantage point of thought, which is always dual, we construct the search as our meaning. We are like the rat that sees its movement through the maze as given purpose by the resulting food. It is perfectly logical from the thought perspective. But thought is only a mechanical process conceptualizing life; it is not life itself. Thought cannot access totality, but totality has the capacity to move through thought. Although in language we talk about the relative and the absolute, there is really only singularity.

No One Meditating

Is meditation necessary?

The challenge of meditation has to do with the disassociation that takes place with the development of a watcher (the one who is aware). Meditation generally seems to relieve a certain tension for many people, but it also seems to create a subtler problem. First, we're in pain. Then we meditate and become "aware" of the pain. That certainly feels better. The mind captures this so-called awareness and creates a watcher who feels better because it is aware of the conditions of life. But the watcher is not in actual contact with these conditions. It stays back at a safe distance.

Let's renounce the watcher and awareness. Now we collapse back into the actuality of our life, pain and all. Back, by the way, to where we began and where we are. We are no longer disassociated by the cultivation of watcher-awareness, but rather we are enmeshed in the sometimes grueling facts of life.

There is also a tendency to associate the movement of our lives with the things we are "doing," as if they are causative. We sit in meditation, and something happens. Perhaps it is the opening that causes the meditation, or perhaps it is acausal or synchronistic, but the mind tends to structure, to remember events as causal, and thereby obscure the actuality.

I think I understand your point about techniques. But the peace that I've felt during meditation is like nothing I've experienced before. How can you just throw it out completely? Do you think there is any use for meditation, perhaps as a tool for relaxation? My practice now revolves around the decision to be content with my suffering, even love it. Is it the same thing you are talking about?

Certainly, meditation has technological uses. It appears to relax us, lower the blood pressure, increase concentration, and perhaps bring about changes in brain chemistry and functioning. I would suggest that meditation has no use, however, when it comes to fundamental transformation. This is the point at which technology of any sort, including meditation or other psycho-spiritual techniques, becomes useless. Meditation in actuality is the expression of an open inquiry, not the means to any end. If meditation as technology is not discarded here, then it becomes drug-like, and it functions to produce a state that we feel is pleasurable, valuable, or socially constructed as "spiritual." We will simply repeat the meditative process, get the high, come down at some later time, and repeat the cycle. This is better than drug addiction, but not really much different in substance.

Pain and conflict are messengers. Discomfort transforms as resistance dissolves and open listening occurs. The message emerges, as pain and the resisting self merge into silence.

I am laughing and will be laughing for a while. I've been doing Zen practice and my wife says I've become a zombie. She's right. What you are saying has struck chords that have never been struck before. I never realized how hard a person could be on himself. Now I think I will be spending more time with her, not traveling an hour and a half just to learn another concept.

The wives are usually right.

You don't put much faith in negating thoughts, but I believe that if one practices this diligently, the ego gets steadily weaker, and a point comes where it disappears. This method does not produce a dramatic loss of ego, but a slower, less traumatic loss.

The chipping away of the ego that you describe brings about relative change. But how can it bring about fundamental transformation when the one who is chipping away is the actual problem? You have the idea that the self can do something about its condition, which is the fundamental illusion. Is there a traumatic loss of self outside of the social construction of such? Of course, that can seem pretty traumatic.

Through my practice of negating thoughts there came periods of acute consciousness several times per day, sometimes lasting hours. This consciousness put my ordinary state of mind to shame. The quality of this consciousness slowly changed over a few years to the certainty that I was absolutely in the present, here and now. This changed again to its present quality of "no one doing and acting." More time is required before I would call it a fundamental transformation. These qualities came of their own accord, and seem to demonstrate what you say is an impossibility, that practice can lead to the loss of self.

Why do you believe that there is a causal link between your practice and the states that you describe? What is the nature of the organization of "the way it was" and "the way it is" into a continuous entity? How do you know that the state of mind changed and not the describer of these states? Is there a difference? This past, which is memory and thought, conditions the present. We then struggle to free ourselves from that conditioning. The attempt to be free and the measurement of how well we are succeeding is itself the conflict.

Even in mindfulness meditation, the tradition in which I was trained, this sense of trying to fix something exists. Even though I try to be aware of it, I am being aware of it in order to fix it.

You're constantly trying to fix yourself, and in doing so, you're actually creating the problem. When you see that complete loop, then you're just left holding the paradox. That's all. There's nothing to do with it. It's a state of beingness that makes most of us very uncomfortable. Just *be* with a condition that's not broken and not fixable—and imperfect.

Being with the paradox may have its own sense of dynamic tension, but it's not going to hurt. Nevertheless, I think it's going to hurt, so I avoid it.

That presents another question, which is, "What does it mean to hurt when the hurt is psychological?" It's not a broken leg; it's a mind telling itself that it hurts. The mind refers to memory and says, "This happened then and so it is either happening now or will happen; therefore I need to be in conflict." You have to try to fix the hurt for it to seem real. But doing nothing about the hurting changes the dimension in which it exists. Not that it disappears, but it doesn't collect our "doing" energy around itself. The doing function, then, is no longer reflective of this idea of "me," which *is* pain. It expands into a relationship with all of life.

The doing function begins to express itself as life, not as me. This is where I think a transformed world begins, in terms of the structures of reality. Until this occurs, the only structures we'll have are the same old forms again and again. It's an entirely mechanical process. It doesn't have anything new in it. It's a closed system that doesn't allow anything new to occur.

Teachers and the Path of Imitation

I am looking for a teacher to help me remove some obstacles from absolute realization. Can you help me?

Why do you think there are obstacles?

All right, there are no obstacles. But being "enlightened" does not mean that one has completely integrated this into one's whole being, to the point where it is experienced without breach. What kind of practice do I need to do to integrate my enlightenment fully into myself?

I have no interest in being a teacher, so I can't be of help to you there. I am very interested in exploring the actuality of life as the ideas of spirituality fall away and nothing replaces them. This expresses itself out of great intensity, humility, and honesty, which either you have or you don't.

Deconstruct all the assumptions you are making about enlightenment. Who gets enlightened, anyway? Who is the subject of the objective reality? What have you assumed about "practice" as a method to find freedom? How would you know you are integrated? Is it a state? Is there panic if it ever disintegrates?

Let me know what you discover.

I know your books must be hitting home with those who have been meditating for a while, but have you met anyone who was never influenced by Eastern philosophy who understands what you're trying to get across?

I have no way of measuring what anyone gets. It does seem to me that the person who has practiced materialism and the person who has practiced spirituality are not fundamentally different.

After a few years of studying Buddhism, following that well-worn path of spiritual imitation and consumption, I chanced upon some of J. Krishnamurti's writings. I realized after reading them that the search I was undertaking was a useless quest. How does Krishnamurti's work relate to yours?

Krishnamurti, from what I know of him, had a great interest in the exploration of life as it is. In this we can all find kinship with him. I don't attempt to relate what I am to what he was in any way, which is perhaps the greatest honor that can be paid to his life's work. After all, the discovery of the silence in each of us in each moment is the intelligence that is shared.

Why do spiritual teachers seem to end up in scandal?

Transparency in the world of spirituality is long overdue. It's time for the financial books to be open, the structural and hierarchical books to be open, and for the power and sexual structures to be open. We demand that in our intimate relationships, but we don't demand it of our teachers. This is where we really put our lives into someone else's hands, but we never really challenge or question them.

Unfortunately, a certain dynamic in most of these situations prevents such open examination. Given all the scandals that have occurred in the past few years, it should be clear that we need a different way of understanding the student-teacher relationship. I'm suggesting that the whole hierarchical structure is inherently corrupt.

It seems to me that followers often condition the leader. Followers are looking for someone to tell them there is a "there" and that they know how to guide them to it.

Each needs the other. It's so much more interesting to create a relationship of freedom, autonomy, and mutual responsibility, because that's where this rich dialogue can take place. That's the only way we can access the fullness of human wisdom. A single biological instrument, and all it can perceive, is not enough. It's not enough in terms of the transformation of the human condition. Nor is it enough to change the structures of society and create new forms that reflect the inherent holism of life.

The forms we have now express division, the ideas of ego, and the conceptualization of survival. But we are each conducting an experiment. Can we find structures that actually reflect our commonality?

Hierarchy produces the same old story over and over again. We already know it doesn't work. We can't go down that road because we've been down it before and we know where it leads. And even though we don't know what's next, we're willing to try something new.

"Not knowing" is actually the intelligence we need. Once we know what's next, in the sense that we are able to lay out the whole pathway, we've just created a new philosophical system. No philosophical system can hold a life that is vital and changing and fully energetic.

So let's begin to imagine and live the forms that have the flexibility to move with life. That's the real challenge of the human condition. Once we've put aside these ideas of fixing ourselves, of completing the spiritual journey, then we can actually have the journey of life as it presents itself to us.

There are gurus who may know this, yet instruct their disciples to do practices anyway. What motivates that?

Gurus are having an experience of no thought, or bliss, which is attractive. Given that they have come to their experience through a teaching, a background, a guru of their own, they are conditioned about what they're supposed to do with that experience in relation to other people. Some of them are clearly interested in power. They know how to produce these experiences in their own brain cells, and perhaps they even know how to transmit them.

If I'm Steven Spielberg and I can show you a movie that takes you to a distant galaxy and makes you feel all kinds of things, then you'll give me money and power. That's a gross form of the same kind of teaching. If I'm a teacher who makes you feel happy, you'll give me a lot.

There is often a lack of integration in the teacher. Eastern teachers may come to this country unprepared for our culture. What they find here blows them away. They can sit very still and project certain qualities, but they're not socially or emotionally integrated.

What the seeker looks for becomes the expression of the projection. Most people want a state of no thought. You can sit on a cushion and focus your thoughts into one little area of your mind so that everything else becomes inert and damaged. Is that what we're really looking for? Or do we want to find full contact with the actuality of life? If full contact is what we want, we're already there.

So is the spiritual journey like the line from William Blake, "A fool who persists in his folly becomes wise"?

Perhaps it's more that a person who pursues his wisdom becomes a fool. Socrates said that the only true wisdom is to know that we don't know. That's the fact for anybody who has the integrity to look at how his world is constructed. No matter how much we can accumulate, we still don't know. As much information, history, and experience as we can pile up, we still don't know.

What has been your experience over the years as you've shared your work with others?

It's a difficult kind of exploration. It's very challenging to question one's life. There's no particular result that should come out of this. It's not that you should hear what I've said and do something or become something from it. As I explore my own life, I find it's important to communicate with those around me. I don't need to change anybody and I don't need anybody to respond in a particular way.

What moves you to reach out and communicate?

Communication is an inherent quality in life. It represents the actual interconnectedness of life. It's a manifestation of that interconnectedness. It's not really my communicating to you, it's the manifestation of our relatedness. That's why the form that seems most obvious to me is that of dialogue rather than of teaching. I am decidedly not teaching anything to anyone.

Do you have any full-time students who are engaged with you in an ongoing and intimate way? Do you even offer this?

I don't offer anything and I don't teach anyone. There isn't anything to do about being; we are already doing it. The recognition of that, the acceptance of the full responsibility of our lives and the relationship to everything, is the very nature of this being. That is not the end point of a spiritual search. That is the beginning of the inquiry into the nature of life.

Isn't life about communion and communication? For me, this means contact with the world around me, and the expression of my perception. I have books out. I give talks around the world. I meet with individuals. We have a charitable organization that works with destitute children and provides medical care in Asia. Some of us participate in a living community and an alternative school. The life of this community and its projects is a laboratory where we can see more about life as a social construction. This is a vital part of exploration and tests the words we speak against the life we live.

Anyone who is interested in this life of intensity is welcome to share it, to find an expression in his or her relationship to me. I invite that direct involvement. But this is not a requirement or a necessity, and I can hardly see why anyone would do so. I am promising absolutely nothing, and I guarantee that I will deliver on that promise.

Enlightenment on the Night Shift

As I explore, it seems that my central motive is to attain this thing called enlightenment. I read spiritual books or I stop reading them. I try to live with full attention to the moment, but it just makes me tense. I read the Advaita sages. Now I have got it. I am already free. I remind myself of my already-free state. I inquire as to the nature of my self. I notice that there is a constant awareness through all states, and all things arise and disappear in this awareness. I do nothing. All in an attempt to get this thing called enlightenment. None of it works. I get clever. I give up all seeking, but then I look to see if anything has happened. Am I enlightened yet?

I have never clearly questioned if enlightenment even exists, or considered that it could be a myth—just a more sophisticated version of trying to get to heaven. If enlightenment is truly a myth, then what would my life be about? What is the way to freedom?

This is precisely the exploration. What is our life about? You have discovered a few layers, but upon seeing this, those layers lose meaning and something else emerges. This is not a dilemma; this is a vital life unrestrained by a conditioned goal. Perhaps some other conditioning emerges to replace the old, or perhaps something that is unconditioned is possible. This is the unknown; no one has a map.

All my questions are variations of "How can I get enlightened?" That there is no enlightenment is a great relief. It is also, if I am honest, a bit of a disappointment. It is a compelling fantasy. I am left with a sense of questioning, with a feeling of "I just don't know." I am left with just this moment. I am looking for a certainty that does not exist. What is this question

I am left with? Is there an answer? If there indeed is no enlightenment, so no need to search for it, why do I continue my questions?

The end of enlightenment seems to express itself as an ongoing dialogic inquiry. It requires an openness, creativity, and attentiveness to the actual, which is fresh in each moment, but which cannot occur in separation.

Why do you claim enlightenment is a myth? How do you view historically enlightened people? Are they charlatans?

The whole spiritual world is mythic. The historic figures are mythic. The individuals who claim these states are mythic. They may believe in and become absorbed in those myths. Myths are powerful communication tools and so they're very useful in building organizations and the whole material aspect of spiritual teaching.

Do you think then that there is an enlightened state?

What would that be?

Perhaps an understanding of the thought process and the ego.

And what would that person have that you don't have?

Perhaps a life free of psychological pain and conflict. Perhaps the ability to go into ecstatic states of divine bliss.

You can do that by taking Thorazine. Then would you be enlightened? If you have a frontal lobotomy, are you enlightened? You are now in an ecstatic state, and you have no problems. People even come and feed you. Are you enlightened? What is enlightenment? Take the enlightened person out of his or her context and see what happens.

Out of their environment, with their followers, their teachings?

Yes. Put them in a convenience store in New York City on the night shift for twelve hours and then see what happens. I don't think that enlightenment exists for these teachers outside the context of the group, the theology, and the belief system. If you're inside that, it's an enlightened state, but that enlightened state exists only with the agreement of the two thousand followers.

And do you equate this scenario with the historically enlightened people?

We know a little about the historic figures, but there's not sufficient information to say anything, really. Scholars get together and talk about fragments of parchments containing stories by disciples of somebody who may or may not have existed. That's useful if you're very interested in that particular religion and the particular individual who was supposed to have started it. It doesn't really tell us much about the state of mind of that individual. These figures don't exist historically. They exist as archetypal representations of certain qualities. Jesus represents an embodiment of compassionate love and Buddha might represent non-attachment. This is symbology or mythology.

Does the fact that their words have lasted all these years speak to anything?

If you come back ten thousand years from now, there will still be Styrofoam containers with the McDonald's logo printed on them. Does that give the McDonald's logo substance? I think religion tells us something about the human psyche.

That it held on to such teachings for so long?

Yes, that the human mind wants a belief system. It wants to have mythic figures. It wants to divide itself from its own potential by projecting a God figure. That potential exists in each of us in this moment. We decide not to accept that because we want our cars, our houses, our stereos, our computers, and the rest of it. That's what we're drawn to.

You suggest that the various modes of spiritual practice that have been used for thousands of years are irrelevant to the discovery of ultimate truth. What practice do you see as valuable in aiding us in this discovery?

No practice is going to aid us in the discovery of ultimate truth. If you understand that enlightenment is a myth, then what practice would you undertake to get enlightened? If the place isn't there, then how do you get to it? The value of these practices is that they give you some technical information about how your mind and body work. That's as interesting as learning about architecture, or mathematics, or art history, but it doesn't result in enlightenment. You can be a master of the workings of the mind, but if you are deluded by your sense of self you will simply use that mastery to manipulate people.

So obviously you don't see any value in petitionary prayer.

Petitionary prayer has no value as a means to becoming enlightened. Does it bring a person temporary relief from pressures that they may be experiencing? Does it calm them? Does it make them feel better? Does it give them a sense of doing something? Probably.

So there's some relative value to the practitioner?

Yes, there's some relative value to everything. Otherwise, it wouldn't exist. We do things because we believe in the connection between "doing" and getting someplace. We repeat those patterns. We pray to God that lightning won't strike our house, and lightning doesn't strike our house. We say, "Hmm, that worked. I think I'll pray tomorrow." So we pray tomorrow. "Please don't let the lightning strike the house." We do that over and over and the lightning doesn't strike. It works, and then five years later lightning *does* strike our house. Now we have to come up with an explanation, and theology is born. Those who can explain why the lightning struck become the priests. The causality of our action, the result of our action, is what has to be questioned.

Why do all these enlightened beings, supposedly beyond any sense of personal doer-ship, still find it necessary to talk about themselves as separate entities? Would a truly non-dual consciousness speak or write, and what would it have to say, and to whom?

Enlightenment is a myth. Non-duality is a story. Aren't these so-called enlightened beings defined as such by those of us who choose to define ourselves as unenlightened? Isn't this a social construction and a mutual delusion?

Language seems to be based on a subject-object relationship, a technological strategy that allows the concrete world to be manipulated. This is useful for biological survival. Thought and language have expanded this subject-object relationship into a psychological world where a created "me" strives to avoid the actuality of its non-existence. This psychological reality is the basis of great conflict, but the conflict is concept, just as the "me" is.

You seem to me to be a teacher in the lineage of Ramana Maharshi. Do you see yourself that way?

Ramana Maharshi had no lineage. He had ample time to create one and did not. He did not even want an ashram. He barely agreed to speak or teach. How then can anyone claim to be in his lineage, and further, what is the motivation to claim this? I have the highest regard for Ramana, and I honor him each day by having nothing to do with him.

What is the measuring stick of integrity regarding a teacher's actions?

All kinds of motivations are floating around in the mind, and to try to sort them out is madness. Integrity is the quality that is actualized in each of our lives, and in the realization that each of our lives is the same as all of our lives. Integrity leaves an imprint on the circumstance that is easily seen. We can just as easily look the other way at the indications of corruption if we are trying to get something out of the circumstance. The corruption in spirituality is not just the teacher using power for control, for sex, for money. It is, at its core, the base materialism of the spiritual search. Any context that reinforces the spirituality of narcissism lacks integrity.

I would suggest that corruption exists in any power-based structure, and spiritual power is no exception. Most people are not interested in seeing this because they are getting what they want from the spiritual structures, just as they do from corrupt political structures.

Recently I have been examining exactly what it is that I am searching for. Perhaps I am looking for some permanent state of certainty, a sense of finally having arrived. If I am honest, there is also a desire to be superior to others: "Now I am one of the enlightened ones, like Buddha."

You have said that the mind wants to dominate. This is surely the case for me. How easy it is to hide our self-centeredness under the guise of spirituality. Even dropping the search for freedom has become projected as another goal to be achieved some time in the future. My mind is often filled with numerous ideas that I have read or heard about how to live life, all in conflict with each other. And yet, in addition, there is the watching of all this mind movement and a quiet at the center of this movement.

From the perspective of thought, everything we encounter, including spirituality, is a concept. Even giving up spirituality is a concept. Silence is a concept. This is the nature of thought. Getting wrapped up in how thought shouldn't be keeps us involved in fixing thought, as if thought were broken. Thought isn't broken. Conceptualizing is what it does;

dividing is its function. In this respect, thought as it is—whatever quality it has, even as concept—is the actuality. We are already in contact with thought-as-it-is.

Perhaps the exploration turns to the nature of the world of actuality (world-as-it-is) rather than the obsession with one aspect of thought changing or fixing another aspect of thought, or the idea of transcendence or freedom from the world. There is a lot of juice in focusing on fixing or transcending. There is no specialness to the world of actuality. And, of course, the notion of teaching someone how to be where she is, is absurd, so there's no power in it either. The only thing that actuality has going for it is that it is actual.

I think of enlightenment as the rabbit being chased by the greyhounds on the racetrack. No matter how hard the hounds run, they're never going to catch the rabbit.

That's right. And if you were a really smart greyhound, wouldn't you stop running?

Do you think it's possible, in some permanent way, to step out of the "me" that's functioning in the world to become a piece of the whole?

The idea of stepping out of something presumes that there's a place that we started from and a place that we're going to. I think that the actuality of our situation is that we're in only one place, which is in fact the universal place. Whether it's a concept arising out of space, or whether it's space itself, that is the universe, that is the contact with the universal, that is the so-called enlightenment. Enlightenment is not a place out there. It's a place where we are, and the only thing that obscures this is the constant movement of concepts. We're not going anyplace. We just have a thought that projects a place we're going to. If there is enlightenment, it is our natural state. We don't need a hierarchy, an authority, a mediation. We don't need someone to interpret the universe for us. It's right here.

But, don't I need a teacher to help me wake up?

We're already awake. We don't have to become awake. Thought attempts to maintain its hold on us through any means possible. One of the great ways of doing that is the regression into a childlike state in which we think, "I'm not awake. I'm asleep and I need you to wake me up." You don't need another person to wake you up. Our relationship to each other can happen only when I don't want anything from you and you don't want anything from me, including enlightenment. It's an autonomous, adult, responsible relationship. That is worth exploring.

Are you suggesting that people simply stop all spiritual seeking immediately?

You can continue seeking if you so desire, but it's recreational spirituality. Perhaps there's no good movie or concert tonight, so I'm going to go hear some spiritual speaker. That's fine, but let's call it what it is. It's recreation, entertainment, a form of social interaction, but it has nothing to do with a movement from an unenlightened state to an enlightened state. It's just a response to our boredom, an attempt to entertain ourselves.

It seems to me that a lot of the searching that makes gurus into all-powerful teachers comes from a basic yearning not to be in the pain in which most humans find themselves.

Searching comes primarily from fear. It comes from the attempt to gain power and control over the context of our life. That's a deal with the devil: I'm going to give my personal power and authority over to you, and you're going to solve my problem. I'll be protected. I won't have to experience the pain, the conflict, the inherent friction of life, the juxtaposition of the relative world and the absolute. But the deal always collapses. We always come back to where we are.

So in the end, are you suggesting that people simply raise their children, cook their soup, dance, and so on? Should they give up the search for more compassion?

No, I'm suggesting that we live our life and that the so-called search become an inquiry. Rather than looking for an alternative state, I'm suggesting that we make contact with the actuality of where we are—all the qualities, the good, the bad, and the ugly, as they're occurring in our life—and ask the simple question, "What is it?" Not, "How do I get away from it, how do I make it better, how do I become something else?" We haven't even discovered what we are yet, so how are we going to know what to do about it, or how to do it? That question is not just "What am I?" It's "What are we?" What are marriage, family, community, and the whole of the human race?

Deconstructing Psychology

I have been neurotic all my life, but have always tried to use my angst in a positive way. Is the neurotic mind immune to existential enlightenment?

All personality is neurotic. Its nature is to obsess on personal survival, which is not a bad thing if you're trying to cross a busy street. Our investigation is not only about the nature of the mind, but of the no-mind that wraps around it. These elements that are apparently two, the neurotic and the still, are in actuality one. The neurotic mind *is* existential enlightenment. This is evident when the idea that it is not (which we have been taught) simply falls away and the bare actuality, whatever its quality, is all there is.

I am a psychologist, and I feel a little like a fraud. I recognize that the problems people offer me are usually efforts to find a solution and continue on the journey of the separate self. How can I assist people without perpetuating their illusion?

The very structures out of which we ideate and carry out our actions are fraudulent. Our concern with survival is a motivator. What does not seem to be as obvious is that we are aware of the fraud, and the fact that we are doing nothing about it. And, of course, that we should be doing something.

This doing nothing, but feeling that we should be doing something, seems like the result of our deep insight, but in fact it is the very problem itself. It is the tension under which we attempt to be whole.

But, it is not through acts that we will discover wholeness, rather wholeness expresses inherently all the time. How could it not? Our feeble attempt to craft better acts obscures this fact.

Can you offer some view on how to stay in my profession? I have been trained to help relieve the pain. I enjoy my profession but want the time with people to be a freeing experience, in the existential sense of the term. How can I remain true to the spirituality in everything and also be a psychotherapist?

Why not make your question the answer and bring it into your work in a transparent way, offering both the band-aid and the deeper resolution to those you work with? Why not make the movement to the band-aid, which is our typical response to pain, part of the exploration of conflict, both in yourself and in the client? Nothing is wrong with relieving pain, but it is mostly done without addressing the cyclical nature of the relief-buildup-relief, or without addressing the more fundamental issues of beingness.

You say the central thought of "me" is the basis of our psychology, yet you say it goes unexamined. Haven't we actually attempted to examine this thought structure through therapy and religion?

No, we have assumed that it's there. That is the basic assumption that psychiatry comes from—that there is a central "me" that needs to be cured, helped, or consolidated. Who is examining whether this "me" actually exists or not? The psychiatric process is a theoretical process, an intellectual process. It's not experiential. The interesting thing about the Eastern meditation approach is that it is directed towards an experiential contact with the qualities of the "me," or thought as it arises. Is there a "me"? If so, what is it? Let's find out about that before we start curing the "me," helping the "me," making the "me" happier, or giving it psychiatric drugs to make it feel better.

So the therapy that we're familiar with looks only at the symptoms as opposed to the origin or root of psychological pain?

Most of the therapies that we're familiar with look at how they can bill insurance companies. That's their first consideration. Does it fit into the handbook of diagnosis that allows the office manager to send a bill and get paid? The second consideration is how does the therapist get through that fifty-minute session without being bored out of his or her mind? So many therapists can hardly stand seeing yet one more needy person. That's the problem with therapy. It's not honest. The therapist is treating a patient as if there were a disease. Find the disease. Demonstrate it. Where is it? There is simply behavior that is okay with the therapist and behavior that isn't. And if it is a physiological aberration, what is therapy for?

So then you're saying these therapies support the illusions of thought?

It's not that therapies support them—they *are* the illusions. If you have the idea of "me," then the "me" by its nature is separate and has to be in pain or in difficulty. Then it has to find its way to feeling better. To feel better you go to a therapist, you go to a priest, you take on a religion, or a philosophy. If you're separate, you're in pain.

And the therapies don't look at that essential aspect of the "me"?

The therapies look at the manifestations, and once you're in that world, you're in an endless world. You go to a therapist and you say, "I'm in pain." If the therapist says, "You're in pain because you're in separation, and you're in separation because every building block of your life is sitting on a false foundation," you have to disassemble your life. You have to go through a complete re-evaluation. People don't go to therapists for that. They go for a fix so that they can maintain their lives. If the therapist is that honest, he or she is out of business. If the therapist is out of business, the therapist has to look at his or her own life. How many are interested in that?

This is a deep question that every practitioner of psychology must face: "Am I allowing consciousness to move fully in my own life?" It's not in the patient; it's in me. And when it's moving fully in me, then it moves in relationship to the so-called patient.

Now we're exploring together; we're back to dialogue. And when I'm in dialogue with the patient, I can no longer stand outside of the "insanity." I have to go into it. If I go into the insanity, then I'm in a different place from the safe and distant practitioner. It's not a safe place, but it's a transformative place.

Though it is true that some psychologies and therapies create problems, many forms do not. The trend for many is to accept the patient's definition of the problem, rather than diagnosing according to a medical model. Problems are behaviors that someone considers undesirable, rather than manifestations of pathology. If no one is complaining about a problem, there is no problem. What do you think?

It seems that psychology as a field has within it those who have deconstructed the social contexts of the "illness" model. My concerns with psychology have to do with the tendency to pathologize existential challenges and at the same time, perhaps, to psychologize physiological imbalance. I would like to see the field of psychology take on questions like: What is consciousness? If there is mental illness, outside of brain abnormalities, where does it reside? Are psychological problems individual issues or societal/collective definitions? If behavior is undesirable, why not make it illegal rather than an "illness"? Does change take place through process or is it acausal? Is it grace? The field of psychology is undergoing great change, as it must. Within that change are some brilliant individuals who are getting at the heart of the matter.

It seems to me that all behavior takes place in, and is inseparable from, the social context of which the field of psychology is a part. People must deal with the norms and values that exist around them. It isn't just that psychology is defining a problem as a problem, but that an individual can be in conflict within himself and with others. The individual is suffering and in pain. The job of the psychologist is to help resolve their dilemma. My patients generally are not interested in enlightenment or understanding the nature of the separate conceptual self. Should they not be helped to relieve their depression, resolve their anxiety, or change their self-defeating habits?

We recognize that we are part of, and co-creators of, social constructions that allow us all to function, which at the same time are the expression of separation and often the worst of human qualities. Within that construction, each of us has a role. If we play our role, we know we are living in only a relative aspect.

In psychology perhaps we know that the problem/solution construct, or the mental illness/cure construct, or any number of others being used now, are in fact agreements to take a role. Supporting that are the feelings of helping or the rationale of our education. The person taking the role of the patient has the idea that he is ill, has a problem, or needs help. As a practitioner, we are in the middle of all this. We can't tell if helping creates the problem, or if helping is the relative response to a relatively real issue.

What happens if we don't try to construct or deconstruct, but simply see the situation as it is? What if we also make its qualities transparent to those who share the construct, the "patients"? Can the contact with each other in all our social constructs become a mutual exploration, whatever the context: doctor/patient, employer/employee, husband/wife/child, etc?

The challenge of this inquiry is that it takes us from the safety of the known, the world as we have all agreed to hold it, into the unknown. From the vantage of the mind, which always likes surety even when its surety is wrong, this can look like things are getting worse.

If the psychological client coming to you has no interest in this inquiry, then you are left with your own exploration, revealing your own constructions relative to this client and your own existential dilemma as to what the fullest expression of your life is in this situation. In the end this self-exploration and the resistance to it are the same as the mutual exploration and the resistance to it.

You have been critical of the way Western psychology has made its project the reinforcement of cultural norms, which it defines as healthy.

Psychology is culturally embedded. It exists to bring people back into mainstream functioning so they can be productive in society. Psychology doesn't recognize the validity of non-productivity.

In the culture of India, they recognize that a part of their population is going to be nonproductive, and that's fine. You have sadhus who are engaged in a wide variety of nonproductive activities. Many of them are very flamboyant. Some of them are naked; some of them have costumes. They're just doing what they're doing and it's not judged or disrespected. In fact, it's revered.

In our culture we have the same kind of people, maybe in homeless shelters, or on the streets, or in mental institutions. Not only are they not revered, they are looked upon as a burden to society.

In some respects, psychology has been co-opted by a viewpoint that doesn't recognize the possibility of spiritual crisis. As consciousness moves from a mind clinging to a bundle of concepts into the recognition that concepts are all relative, there is going to be a great crisis in the individual. All the things that we have built our life around collapse in that moment. But modern psychology generally doesn't recognize these crises as a possibly positive movement of consciousness.

No, it's immediately defined as pathology.

Our whole society is desperately trying to contain its collective angst. We're drugging our students with Ritalin so they'll sit still in school. We're drugging our workers with Prozac so they won't be depressed about going to the factories. And we're drugging ourselves with television and the Internet so we don't have to face our own boredom with our life. Our culture is trying to restrict something that cannot be contained, and that is the movement of consciousness. For psychologists, perhaps the more accurate response is to become like a shaman, to become a midwife of this transformation.

People who come to me as a psychotherapist are in pain and struggling. I have been experimenting with suggesting that they don't need to do anything about their emotions or about their thoughts. I describe the nature of thought. For most, the idea of "doing nothing" is very confusing, though some seem to get it with good results. Any thoughts on this?

The primary issue to be resolved early on is what the "client" wants, that is, what the contract is between the two of you and whether you can provide that. If the client wants to feel better, and that is all, then in some cases a referral to someone who will give techniques or medication would be in order. If the client wants to "understand," then there are resources you can make available to give the individual some perspective. If the client wants "fundamental change," then there is a different response.

Doing nothing addresses fundamental change and perhaps a bit of understanding, but is not necessarily a response to wanting to feel better or to maintain order in a person's life. In many respects, the question is for you to see what you can and cannot do in relationship to the individual. I am not a therapist, but I am seldom able to respond to anyone outside of either a practical, concrete suggestion—such as change jobs, exercise, clean up your diet—or a mystical, transformative perspective, which is essentially to do nothing, and recognize that the personal is only conceptual.

There is obviously a large middle ground where an individual is grappling with psychological issues that are clearly conceptual but nevertheless have the appearance of reality. I have not found that I can be useful to someone in this realm, other than to suggest they find someone else to talk to. To me, this area is one where we can only modify, using fixes that work for a while, using aspirin rather than getting to the cause of the headache. However, for a skillful practitioner, there may be a response to such a situation that addresses the apparently acute crisis, but also recognizes that the transformative work is still there when the metaphorical headache is relieved.

The question also remains whether interfering with a crisis is also interfering with a healing, or for that matter, whether interfering with anything is useful.

Perhaps a middle ground might be this. A person is having obsessional thoughts that they are fighting and resisting. Their solution to the thoughts that they label as unacceptable is to oppose them. By getting them to do nothing about those thoughts, or perhaps by getting them to intentionally think them, they fade out, because there is no resistance.

In addition, it seems that many symptoms are formed as a response to thoughts, feelings, and impulses that people find unacceptable. The psychological self creates, or is, an idea of who we are. Anything that does not fit our self-concept, our description of how we are supposed to be, creates conflict. The difference between the description and the actuality is often resolved by repression, denial, etc. It seems to me that if we help people to do nothing about their thoughts and feelings, allow them to be as they are, and open up the opportunity to directly experience the bare actuality of their lives without interpretation, most of what we call psychological problems may clear up.

The understanding that life is change—that our attempts to cling to some notion of how it should be or to repeat some past memory are unworkable—would be useful for people to have. People have a tendency to see their problems as unique. As they shift to seeing them as human problems, there is a reduction in the sense of isolation. That which formerly caused isolation now links us with everyone. Would you consider these perspectives a useful middle ground?

One concern that comes up is, let us say that I do nothing and some violent or terrible thought arises, and with it great compulsions and feelings to act. Obviously, if I do nothing, then these tendencies are left without any energy to manifest and they remain as thoughts, without substance. But, the quality of being overwhelmed by these impulses, or the inability to act with kindness or compassion, is usually the issue, along with feelings of sadness and disconnection.

Perhaps the middle ground has more to do with describing the socially constructed parameters, while directing the individual to a more spacious relationship to their own thoughts: don't act on your violent thoughts, as this will get you arrested; control yourself. And by the way, whose violent thoughts are these? What is a thought? What compels you to act on it? What is the relationship between a thought and an action?

Recognizing the impersonal nature of thought forms is essential. The fundamental issue is not the thoughts or the apparent compulsion to act, but rather the narcissism that constructs the whole array as "me." This contraction misses the point that the transformation isn't of my consciousness, but of *all* consciousness, that there is no issue other than the movement of fear/contraction into the space of consciousness/expansion. The challenge is to introduce this in a way that shifts the perspective from that of thought/me to awareness/us. This is a very critical synthesis that has to occur for therapy to be truly useful.

It seems that what you are suggesting as useful is to make a distinction between thought/feeling and behavior. We need do nothing about thought/feeling. It arises spontaneously and disappears in the empty space of consciousness.

There is no need for control here. Behavior, on the other hand, has consequences for ourselves and for others. To feel angry is not a problem. To hit someone might be. Further feeling may be just dysfunctional, conditioned thought forms that arise, in which case we need do nothing about them. Feeling may, however, point to something we need to do or respond to in the world. Winter is coming; my tires are old. A thought arises as to the potential danger. There is nothing to do about the feeling. However, there may be something to do about the tires.

Can you say some more about the construction of a "me"? By this do you mean our idea of a self, as in a self-image or concept, or do you mean the process of identifying thought/feeling as "me"? Are we pure awareness, that which observes the whole show, or is it awareness that is aware of us?

The quality of awareness and thought/feeling are aspects of wholeness, much as two sides of a coin are faces of one thing. Thought, in thinking about this, makes the differentiation into a substantive reality. Awareness, in attending to these two aspects, makes them whole (this is its nature after all) and makes the non-differentiation into a unified reality. The sense of "me" comes from the thinking aspect, which always needs a subject to objectify the world.

We generally believe this is what we are. We keep ourselves busy with the thought-generated aspect. What, in fact, we are is not this thought-me, nor is it pure awareness (whatever that is), but rather the collapse of these aspects into one, much like the wave/particle of quantum physics, which is one thing behaving in different ways. In this respect, what we are is not A or B, but AB. AB is "what is" before it is differentiated and after it is differentiated. This integral vantage, inclusive of the aspects but not identified with either one, is what we are in actuality.

I have experienced severe depression and anxiety for most of my life. I quickly realized that psychiatrists and therapists were not able to help in the least (at least not the ones I have met), and thus began searching and reading for myself. Self-help books led to new age books, which led to years of serious spiritual practice. I realized that with all my "knowledge" of spiritual things I was no better off than I had been before. So I gave up. Then I started to see that the part of me I always thought I was, was being taken apart, and I got scared! And so I fought my way out again. Ever since then, I have been conflicted about returning to that state and have been too scared to risk the self for the Self.

The question has to do with what your relationship is to the experiences you are having. If one were to characterize those experiences as depression, then with that notion comes a whole slew of concepts and helpers to reinforce the notion. In a sense, there is no depression without this social construction, although there may still be some kind of phenomenon. This construction becomes all the more complicated to understand, and still there is the underlying experience—whatever that is—that has to be penetrated. You understood all this and set out in a different direction.

But, is the direction really different? Has the world of psychology been replaced with spirituality, the practitioners of the medicine of mind replaced with the gurus? Where the doctor couldn't fix us, do we look for the spiritual teacher to help?

This takes us back to the original question: What is the relationship to your experience? If it is to change the experience into something else, even if it is from "self" to "Self" (whatever that is), the movement is still the movement of dissatisfaction, restlessness, and getting better. This movement is the creation of time and process, and in time there can be only the projection of timelessness, not the actuality. The projection of the transcendental state is the avoidance of the actuality, the movement away from the perceived collapse, darkness, and pain.

The light is the creation of the darkness, in the world of thought.

If the relationship to the experience is to change it, I would suggest working with both psychologists and doctors and whatever spiritual teachers you can find who have some integrity. In this case, there are basic things you can also do, which will have general effects on experience: diet, exercise, sunlight, friendships, volunteer work, etc.

The problem with seeking bliss is that you have to live in non-bliss in order to seek bliss. When you find bliss, it is ruined by the fear of losing it, and eventually the fact of losing it. But, is bliss the point?

Another relationship to experience occurs when we are, for whatever reason, no longer interested in altering the experience but simply interested in its actuality. This is not really a relationship to the experience, nor is it really an experience. It is the "what is" of any phenomenon, without the interpretation of the conceptual self and without any notion of changing it. We can inquire into the nature of life in this world, we may even experiment with altering the qualities that are occurring. But, the idea of getting better in this relationship to experience is simply an idea.

In actuality, there is no Self, or self, or bliss, or non-bliss, or anything else to go in or out of. This is all thought dividing the universe into two with concepts. Why would I want to experience only part of the universe, when the whole is available, free and present? You and I reside there all the time, because there is no other place—in actuality—to reside.

But, don't you already know all this?

If the psychological self is the source of our problems, both internal and external, and there is nothing we can do to change, transcend, or get rid of the psychological self, then how can we attain freedom? Or does freedom not really exist, except as an idea created by thought, looking for a solution?

Who would we be without our problems?

Some teachers talk about ego as a path, rather than as pathology. You're really saying that ego is pathology.

No, I'm saying that the attempt to *fix* the ego is pathological. I'd say the attempt to do anything with it is pathological. This is where the language of doing nothing comes in. Can we simply look at what it is without attempting to fix it? And does that in some way change our relationship to the so-called ego? Because once I've got an ego and am trying to fix it, I've simply slathered layer after layer of concepts onto something that we're not even sure exists.

What if I do the opposite? What if I do nothing about this thing called the ego? Let's say I'm an arrogant guy. I'm prone to anger, I'm a lousy communicator, and I'm tense all the time. I can try to fix that through any number of techniques, or I can do absolutely nothing about it. What if that is the entirety of the universe—my anger, my tension, my lack of communication? What happens then? What happens if that's all there is? Does that fundamentally change the space in which I can work with my own experience?

As you describe it, it sounds frightening to me.

It's terrifying! We don't have an escape route. And the whole process-oriented world is about an escape route. It's not about dealing with ourselves. It's about *not* facing ourselves by creating time, by creating process. If I can sit another retreat, or go to another seminar, or read another book, then I'll be able to fix everything. Of course it never works. We just get farther and farther away from the truth.

What if the world is only the fact of what we are? What happens if I am only anger and there is no escape? Now I have a different universe to explore, don't I? Now I get to explore what anger actually is. And I will discover that anger isn't what the psychiatrist described to me or what the workshop leader talked about. It's an occurrence that has certain qualities. It moves in certain parts of my body, and triggers certain kinds of feelings and memories, which all exist right now. Only now.

In this moment, we have stepped out of time, we're out of location, and we're in a transformational universe. At this moment, anger becomes energy. It's only when we blow that moment up into time and concept that it becomes anger. Then it is hooked into us in a way that makes it permanent.

In other words, when we simply experience it in the moment, it's not a problem.

It's not anything. But as a concept, you've got a problem to fix.

And the fixing of it isn't really fixing it at all. In fact, it's creating the "problem" that appears to need fixing.

Exactly. This is the whole Alice-in-Wonderland world that psychology and spirituality have created.

The Heart of Being

The Heart of Being

For the listener, who listens in the snow,
And, nothing himself, beholds
Nothing that is not there and the nothing that is.
—Wallace Stevens

The mind creates a conceptual framework that misdirects us from the fullness of our world, our life, and our relationships. The ideas of enlightenment, spirituality, psychology, and therapy—all the process-oriented approaches to understanding—are problematic, because they move through time. They are always taking us outside of where we are into a potential future that we can call enlightenment or resolution. Let us challenge the concepts of spirituality and therapy, the idea of enlightenment. Let us move through words into silence, into the moment.

Silence is the space or the ground out of which our entire conceptual world appears to arise. It is what we normally think of as the background. But, is it? Or is it the foreground? Silence is not what our self arises out of, but what our self is.

We make the very quick presumption that we've been conditioned to make, that what exists is me and you. There is the observer—me—and the phenomenon that I am observing—you. That is a presumption that we seldom question.

I am not suggesting that nothing exists. Something exists and we're trying to understand what that is. The first clue we come to is this dualistic language—me and you—which we learn from a very early age. Look past the structure of language and discover how the universe is actually built. The location of awareness is not findable.

So perhaps you think, "Well, at least I have a body—that's who I am." But quantum physics describes the material world in such a way that you can't find the location of a particle. So either way you go, either internally or externally, you can't really find a location, and yet we have this embedded concept of "me," which describes a definite location. This "me" doesn't seem to be working very well. It's the basis for our societal and personal structures, which are conflicted and creating a lot of damage.

Once you've heard that, throw the words away. Don't take these words, which are simply the attempt to communicate with symbols that which is fundamentally non-symbolic, and make them into more than they are. These symbols do not need to implant themselves in our memory as something other than what they are. What we're looking into is something of a fundamentally different nature.

Investigate "being" rather than "doing." We are a culture that *does* naturally. We are great doers. We can destroy forests, build huge cities, take over whole continents. We've proven that we can do, but we haven't proven we can be. In our culture there's little respect for being, for the simple act of existing. When you meet someone they say, "What do you do?" They don't ask, "What qualities are being expressed in your life?"

How do we take the perspective of the question into our lives? How do we live? How do we form our relationships, raise our children, create community, and discover an integral perspective, a spirituality that is beyond belief? Let us examine some of the possibilities for a life structured around exploration and connection, rather than competition and survival, where information is recognized as a tool of technology, but not a description of the fullness of life.

When, as a culture, we accepted belief as relative, we also gave up the coherence of a society where standards of ethics and morality are provided. What guides us in this brave, new, post-modern world?

We just can't believe it. We've tried the churches and the synagogues, the meditations and the masters, the channelers and the chanting. We tried it all. And we just can't believe it.

This is postmodern spirituality. It's beyond belief.

We're not cynical; we've just been there and done it, and we're still here. Same life. Same me. Not cynical, just experienced.

The problem is that we want some answers to life's questions. We want to find something that gives us meaning and anchors us in life's churning waters. For our parents, the answer was belief: God, country, and hard work. But we have a problem. God is dead, but spirit is alive. Country defines a political fact, but not a spiritual ideal. Hard work often seems more like our cultural response to uncertainty than the expression of our collective heart.

The societal structures that may have given us surety in the past are either gone or less stable. The ascension of science has altered our sense of mystery. The glorification of violence and sexuality has brought us to the near annihilation of taboos and engendered the sense that we are capable of anything—the most outlandish, the most horrible, and worse. The concentration of wealth in our society has raised materialism to a new ideal, overshadowing our concerns for community and cooperation. Computer technology and the Internet have made all information immediately available at all times. Space and time are merging into a super-infonova of virtual reality.

We know too much to believe in anything. We have an oversupply of information and an unfulfilled demand for credibility. We long for the missing element, the catalyst that will give meaning to the message. In a world where content is just the vehicle for commerce, commerce the means to wealth, and wealth the expression of our value, we have come to feel that our lives are without purpose, without connection, without grounding. This world of separation is maintained by the motion of our lives, perpetuated by the distraction and busyness that ultimately translate into a life of tremendous stress.

If we stop, even for a moment—this moment—we experience a

profound and fundamental question. This question does not look for an answer; it looks beyond all answers. We come to it in the silence from which all our answers arise. This question is the stirring of our life, the remembrance of our heart. The world as we have constructed it, with all its pressures and constraints, recedes into a vast space of unknowing as we look into the presence of this very moment. The answers, the conclusions, the assumptions with which we navigate our life, begin to crumble as we hold the question.

It is not an intellectual question we have come to, but rather the expression of beingness and freshness—the joy of inquiry. Although a conscious life is not fundamentally materialistic, it has quality, effect, and responsibility. The nature of consciousness, after all, is inclusive, and as such, ultimately responsible and responsive.

The question to life's answers is the explosion of the heart. It is the demand that we create our lives from an integral perspective, from a query responding to each answer, from the wholeness of silence, answering the limitation of thought.

The End of Effort

I often feel the fact of my life is that I am nothing, aside from a collection of ideas and conditioning. That is both a relief and a shock, but how do you explore nothing?

Are we here to find out something about nothing, or to find out something about the dilemmas in our life and the forms in which we actually move? Nothingness seems to be something that we can find refuge in as a state, as the negation of the forms that are so conflicted. But is that really what nothingness is? Or is nothingness something? Is it something that is active and dynamic, that creates and moves through form, through our lives?

We can get to nothingness, we can touch the absence of a conceptual framework, but can we live it? And, I think a deeper question is, *will* we live it? There's so much about the structures of our lives that tells us it's not possible, it's not convenient, it's not likely. No one else is doing it. So, in the end, we can have a virtual spirituality in which we talk and discover and hear about "nothing." Spirituality then becomes a metaphor for something we will never live. Or we can attempt to live it, in which case we become nothing. And life, the force, the energy, the collective totality, becomes the animating energy of our world. The risk, of course, is that no one else is doing it. There's no reference point. We cannot find other people to imitate. This is risky indeed.

Perhaps there are other people who are living this life out of nothingness, but how would we know that with certainty?

We don't know.

That "not knowing" is actually the guide.

But what we try to find as a guide is "knowing." This teacher looks like somebody who knows something about nothing. And they're living like this, so that's how I should live. But where nothing guides my life, there is no reference point. It's not loneliness, but it is aloneness.

Is that something we can bear? If we can bear it, should we do that joyfully, and proclaim it, and begin to let it be what our life is? And if we can't, shouldn't we stop pretending?

The way we're structured is towards effort, to try and get things. Effort is useless in regard to transformation. When we look at that, what we imagine is a kind of void-state, in which I give up my effort. And then there's the nothing, and nothing is something that we hear so much about.

What is actually left when I give up my effort is a tremendous amount of energy. It's just not mine. It's a dynamic quality; it's not a static quality.

But, we don't think of it like that at all. We think of it as something that is simply inert. What we've created is a state that we can visit when we're stressed. We have to go to work, we have to deal with our kids, we have to pay the bills, because life has demands. It's easy to find that state of rest as a kind of sedation. I go about my stressful life. When it's too much, I access this quiet place that I've learned to get to through my teacher, my books, my practices. I've found a neural pathway to nothing. And then, when I'm okay again, I come back out and get re-stressed. I'm enabling myself to live a conflicted life.

What about abandoning both the conflict and the resolution? What about abandoning the whole way of organizing the world as if it's about me? Whether I feel good or not. Whether I like what you say or I don't. Whether I feel happy or sad.

We sort the universe into these two categories. We try to enhance the qualities that we like and we try to escape the ones we don't like. We've discovered in nothingness something that helps our lives feel better. But, getting *my* life working better does not necessarily help *life* work better.

What we usually call effort and what we call the state of nothing are both the same thing. They're both ideas. But something else is active, dynamic, moving through our life. It is neither our effort nor our effort to be effortless. It is only empty in that it is empty of us.

I'm looking for advice on how to trust. Or should I just accept my fear, and let whatever happens, happen? Is this just the way it is?

When you hear the philosophy that everything in life is perfect just as it is, does that mean it's over? Are you done? Are you just a machine, living out its bio-existence, because everything is perfect? If you believe that, then you're left with that perfect, automatic sorting of "I like, or I don't like."

Or can you perceive the world as something dynamic, changing, moving, in which you are automatically part of that movement? That dynamic is what's perfect, not any particular state, not the conditions in which we find ourselves, but the fact that consciousness is transformative. What this energy of life touches, changes. We are not different from that life energy, or its unitary expression. That's what's perfect.

If you believe, "Okay, it's just going to happen; everything's predestined. It's all a unitary universe anyway; there's no self," then that philosophy satisfies you. If something else is moving in you, then it's moving. What is the urgency for you? What is the dynamic?

The being is moving. But I don't trust that I would be safe if I just go where I'm moved. I could end up anywhere, anyplace, doing anything. That's scary.

It's *not* safe.

But then how can you make that jump? How can you let go completely in a world that's not safe?

You see this immensity moving through your life, and you see this fragmented bundle of thoughts, conditionings, and ideas, which is inherently painful.

And I can see everyone else's now, too.

Everyone else's is also a part of yours, because there's a social contract going on. All the fragments have, in a broken sort of way, agreed to respect the other fragments. You also see that the bundle of thoughts, the "me," doesn't think it will survive.

Well, it might survive, but it's going to be really hard. You might end up in Calcutta like Mother Theresa, or you could end up doing anything.

You could end up working at the cash register at K-Mart, completely obscure. That's the worst—not to be Mother Teresa, but to be nobody, and to not be able to explain it to anybody. Who would understand it anyway? You already are nobody; you're just an idea. And the idea says, "I'm not going to survive."

Now you can see something about yourself. The small self—this bundle of ideas—understands that it doesn't actually exist. Contact with wholeness brings about terror, because it brings about recognition that everything that I've built my life around is unreal. So now this fragmented bundle of ideas called "me" suggests that it's afraid and it can't trust life.

I choose to stay in control because it seems safer.

You think you have a choice in that matter. You believe you can either stay in control, or give up control. The choice itself is an illusion. It is the illusion of thought. Thought posits that it is the chooser, but it is mechanical.

The small self is simply thought, arising with the idea of the thinker. Coincident with each thought is the thought of a thinker, because of the way thought structures itself as a subject in relation to objects. That's all you are. We refer to that as the context, and then we talk from that and through that and about that. In the middle of all this we ask the question, "How do 'I' allow life to move?" You may notice that life is moving, whether you think about that or not, whether you think you control it or not. So something else is moving, and this dynamic whole, this quantum potential is the chooser.

There is free will, but it's not your free will.

That dynamic whole is somewhere in the background. I can't just go there at will.

Thought can't go there at will. Thought doesn't have the capacity to be anything more than what it is, which is fragmented. It can't be whole.

But then do you sit and wait for wholeness to come back?

Well, where is it right now? What can you find right now?

There's the pressure of something wanting to move in, but I'm not letting it. It's wearing on the physiology.

See where the pressure comes from, what resists it, what's on the other side of it. And if resistance doesn't take place, what happens? This is all we have to work with—what is. What is, is not the description of thought, it is the fact as you discover it.

Life is not the state of immensity. It's not the fragmentation of thought. It is both. It's the merger of those two things—both descriptions —into one thing, which is the actuality. You will see this expansion and contraction, this sense of selflessness and self, the undulation of life. If you had no sense of self, you wouldn't take care of yourself. You wouldn't be able to move; you wouldn't function. What good would that be?

You've described it to yourself as an altered state or an alternative state in which self doesn't exist. It's not an alternative state; it is all states. We're investigating everything.

I can't put anything into words anymore.

Just explore that. It's very easy to find confusion, and on the other side of confusion, when you stop describing it as such, is simply life, as it is. It's the fact that thought can't capture life that causes confusion. Then watch as that understanding animates your life. You will get up, you will go someplace, you will do things, and certain things you won't be able to do anymore. When you're in a relationship in which you see the structures of delusion going on, you won't be able to participate in it. Your life changes. It's never *not* been changing. You just started to notice it.

I'm curious whether the state of nothing you're talking about correlates with the Tibetan idea of emptiness and meditation.

Emptiness infusing reality, emptiness in all its manifestations, is what I mean by "nothing." The sense that manifestation is substantial—that is, not empty—gets us into lots of trouble.

Can you get involved with Tibetan Buddhism and not get caught up in the cultural wrappings of it, presuming you are not a Tibetan? If you are a Tibetan, this is just your life. But if you choose Tibetan Buddhism there's just as much richness in that as there is in anything else, if you don't get caught up in the form of things. That would also be true in this dialogue. If we get caught up in the form of things here, then we miss the whole point.

When you say "nothingness," are you referring to an aspect of thought?

We're using words to communicate, and as we use words, we create artificial divisions, such as "thought and emptiness," or "thought and spirit," or "form and emptiness." Our attention deconstructs the language into something that is directly experienced. So, when you go into your direct experience, do you find two things? Do you find thought and spirit? When you talk about examining thought, who is the examiner of the thought? And what is it that embodies the result of that examination?

English doesn't talk about this very well. We have the sense of something, but we don't have the precise language to talk about that experience. We all have experienced the qualities of expansion and of flow, and we all have experienced contraction and conflict.

When I talk about "emptiness," it is the suggestion that thought doesn't have any inherent "thingness" about it. That is, the thought of the chair is not the chair. When I look at you, I see my interpretation of your form, my conditioning, my thought pattern, applied to the actuality of what you are. What we see is not what the world around us is. What we see is our interpretation. This starts at a very young age, because, when you're born and you look around, there's nothing, really. There's no language, there is no chair, because you've never heard the word "chair," you've never learned to speak it.

The way that a baby might organize this room is not the way that you or I would organize it. The baby wouldn't necessarily see a set of 30 chairs with 30 people. It might see eyes, it might just see happy and sad, it might see all kinds of energy qualities, because it hasn't organized itself yet. As the child grows up, he or she may learn what a chair is, as in, "Don't stand on the chair," or "Don't knock the chair over," "Don't spill juice on the chair." So, chairs become more than what they are. They become imbued with all kinds of psychological qualities and feelings. But, the chair doesn't actually hold that.

We don't know what a chair is, actually. This is what's funny. We're living a life as if we know what all these things are, but we don't. A chair may hold a lot of anxiety for me because, let's say, my mother didn't want me to stand on chairs when I was little. The objects in our world have qualities that aren't in the things themselves. Now we take it to a psychological level, where I look at you, and I think, "Do you like me? Do you understand what I'm saying? Or are you just putting up with this dialogue because you don't know if you can leave or not?" I start to interpret all of your body language, all of your presence, in terms of my history. And I can even ask you, "Well, how are you feeling about me?" And you can answer, "I think you're great." Or, "I think you're not so great." Again, I have my interpretation of what those words mean.

We're in this soup of thought, which is not substantial, which is empty. It's only a projection onto the actuality. How do we get to the actuality? How do I meet you? How do I actually know who you are? How do we actually have a relationship? Nobody really knows how to do that.

Language is very useful, technologically. This morning I was asked, "How do you want the room organized?" And I was able to describe, from a remote location, how to set up the room. That's the use of language. It's a technological means of communicating about moving objects. You can move molecules, you can create medicines, you can move steel and make bridges; it's very useful in that regard. It has little use in finding out how to live, how to have relationship, how to make contact with another human being, because all we're seeing is an object we're trying to manipulate. "Your love for me" becomes an object in my mind. "If I can move her in a certain way, she will like me, and I will be happy." That's not the same as moving chairs around in a room, but we think about it as if it is. Those thoughts are empty.

The dynamic quality we've been talking about is the nostalgia for, or the remembrance of, or the fact or actuality of, wholeness and contact with other human beings. We're actually already in contact, but this overlay of technological thought keeps us busy, as if we're not. Religion and psychology are about how to make that technological world work better. How can I be happier, how can I make you like me better, how can I have a better relationship, how can we collectively and socially have a happier world? In some relative way, it works. It's better for us to talk about liking each other than to talk about having war with each other. It's relatively better, but it's not fundamentally different. It's still a virtual world in which we don't have contact.

Can't you use words as a tool for building, especially with regard to feelings, if you're genuine?

Yes, but what the words are building is dangerous. I can say over and over again, "I love you, I love you, I love you," when it's really, "Do you love me, do you love me, do you love me?" Or it's really, "You will love me, you will love me, you will love me." I'm building something, and it seems to be becoming very substantial, but it's becoming a problem, because I don't love you. I love the idea that you'll love me. You can build a whole world around that illusion. We can have a marriage, ten kids, and a whole world that we agree on. But is that really what's going on? I would say it's not. You cannot love me, because you and I are both ideas, and ideas cannot love. Ideas can only have ideas of loving.

There's nothing that you and I can actually have with each other that excludes another person in this room. Only in thought can you do that. I can take "me" and bring "you" into "us," and now we can be separate from, and better than, and happier than the rest. Is that the fact of life?

We are all intertwined in a fundamental way, which we cannot quite get to, because of this burden of conditioning, because we see a roomful of chairs instead of a roomful of life.

To me it doesn't seem like there's the possibility of relationship.

It doesn't seem like it because there's no possibility from this conditioned perspective. There's the possibility of an arrangement with each other, but there's no possibility of actual relatedness. I'm looking at my projection, saying this is somebody I like or don't like. If you're somebody I like, then I want you. And I want you to make me feel good, and we can build a whole social contract around that. But, underlying that is the fact that it's not actual.

I don't know that this swirl of thoughts and conditioning can ever be gone. It seems like that's part of what is.

It doesn't need to be gone. We can build relationships around something besides that. I can go through this room and describe whom I like and don't like based on my conditioning. Each person here can describe whom she likes and doesn't like based on her conditioning.

That sorting is an illusion. It's part of the way we organize our world to survive.

I'm not interested only in people I have an affinity with; I'm interested in all people. In fact, the people I don't have an affinity with generally take me deeper than the people with whom I do. Conflict, which is actually contact with my thought patterns, exposes something about me that peacefulness doesn't.

How do we get a clear idea of what we're experiencing? It seems to me that takes an effort.

If we see that thought is not whole, and effort from thought is not useful, then where could effort come from? There is a kind of movement of energy, dynamic energy, or attention. Where does that come from?

You and I meet today, and we have the potential for being in relationship to each other for the rest of our lives. That happens now. Where does that come from? Will you enter into that relationship now? You can't direct that. The mind will try to figure out, "Is this going to allow me to survive, is this going to be good for me, is this going to be safe?"

Some people in this room will actually enter into a relationship with others in this room for the rest of their lives, whether it's safe or not. And others will think about that, and will go about their lives. Why is that? Where is that coming from?

Can you see within yourself any possibility of having a relationship, or can you only find ways of positioning yourself so that you do okay, so that you survive? And yet, we are here to find that which takes us beyond survival.

There is great energy in this room, but it's not your energy and it's not my energy. We could be doing so many other things. Why are we here? Where does that energy come from? You can find an organizing principle within your brain, which has been trained to move your attention around your body. We've learned that, yes, I can feel my foot, I can feel my hand, I can feel the thought arising. But no one has taught us how to see that organizer. That organizer is incapable of having a relationship, because it's trying to organize relationships. Relationship is inherently dangerous. It cannot be organized. It will destroy us. It will rip us apart.

What do you mean by "relationship"?

I mean the recognition that we are in life. We are in love. We are not in love in the sense that I'm going to get something from you, or that I have something to give you, but we are actually in a field of love. That field is what we are.

Or throw out the word love; we're in a field of emptiness. We're in a field of consciousness. We're in a field of quantum possibility, of interconnectedness. These are all words that carry ideas. But, what we are in is something indescribable, unknowable, that cannot be organized. It's not in the conceptual realm. Would you like to live in that? Would you like to explore that as your life? That's the question for each of us.

Life has tremendous energy. It's not all expressed; much of it is potential energy. It's like the energy in a car battery. You see the potential energy actualizing when you put the cables on and mistakenly touch the ends together and the sparks fly.

The energy is what is making the effort. The resistance is all the thoughts that try to organize us for survival, because that's what thought does, and thought is very, very good at it.

I suppose it's a positive thing, then, that I am confused at this point.

The question that happens in any intense relationship is, "If you don't understand, are you still willing to explore the relationship?" Are you willing to stand still in the midst of confusion, misunderstanding, the thought that this is idiocy, this is confusion, this is craziness?

I've got two teenagers!

Then you know what it means to have no choice. We agree to stand still in the midst of all this. That's what silence is when words stop, and that's what the words are attempting to describe. The stillness in the midst of the motion. The stillness begins to be the director, rather than the organizing principle of thought that says, "Here's how I can survive." That stillness is the effort. Stillness is "efforting." It doesn't make sense, because the concepts of stillness and effort don't go together. That's why it's confusing. But if you are still and simply see, you'll see that stillness is dynamic. That's the quality in which we can live.

The integration doesn't happen in *your* life, it happens in *our* life. You can't integrate your life, because integration has to be whole. That means that this room and other rooms in your life become the context. Your teenagers and other social contexts become the laboratory for integration. I can soothe myself very easily. Go to a nice place in the Himalayas and sit there, and it all feels wonderful. I can be very peaceful very quickly. Great. So what?

Each of us already has a life going on. Let the quality of integration into your life, and let it change your life. It's trying to do that. The only thing that resists it is the idea that it's dangerous, the idea that I won't survive, that it won't look the way it's supposed to look, that I won't recognize myself and people won't recognize me. All of which is likely to be true.

Why Is There Suffering?

Should we do nothing about the suffering in the world?

Psychological suffering is the nature of the relationship between the center and the conceptual reality. Without this abstraction of the actuality there is still pain, but its quality is different.

Suffering takes place in the abstraction and can be "helped" only by the dissolution of the conceptual framework. Anything else is more of the same, since it is still within that framework. Certainly there is modification within the conceptualization, which psycho-technology is very good at, as is religion. These modifications are highly valued and rewarded by society. However, dissolution of the framework requires a response that is not interested in modification, but which addresses the core dilemma of the self and the freedom from psychological suffering. Obviously, most people are not interested in this understanding and will seek out a practitioner who reflects the experience that the "sufferer" is willing to have.

Physical suffering cannot be altered by insight. While it can be understood as the as-isness of the universe, it remains painful. This state requires a response that may help give comfort or alleviation of the pain. This does not deny the unity of the world, but is an expression of it. Averting our eyes at this concrete suffering of another is a trick we play with our no-self philosophy. Of course, if it were our body with the pain, we would do whatever we could to get relief.

Many of us took up our practices—psychological, spiritual, or religious—because we experienced some kind of conflict, some kind of division. We had pain. The question I am posing is: Did the things we took up actually help? Or have they become the pain?

We grew up with so many expectations of how we were supposed to be, and for many of us that was difficult. To understand our difficulties, we took up spiritual practices. We took on new expectations, new ways to be, and new ways to be wrong or imperfect. "Doing nothing" is an expression of what we come to in our own spirituality when the attempt to get better stops.

What happens when we collapse into this moment, where we are, exactly how we are, without any hope, expectation, or anticipation of anything other than what we are? What actually expresses this? What is the potential in our life when we are not using our energy in self-centered, self-serving spirituality? Could we help another human being do something useful? Could we actually be happy?

Is it possible that we're actually okay? Could the expression taking place in our life, innately, without any effort, be the expression of life? Is this the very thing we said we were looking for? And if that is the case, then are we done? And if we are done, then will this be the last "spiritual" book we need to read? Can we go cold turkey? Or will our hands start shaking and will we have to read one more book on how to be enlightened?

Doing nothing is not the collapse of our life into some nihilistic state in which we can't take any action, we're depressed, or we don't know what to do. Doing nothing is the relationship to my own being wherein I can do nothing to change it or make it better.

Find out for yourself in your own life, in your own relationships, who you are and what you are, what "doing" is and what "doing nothing" is. What happens when you try to change yourself? What happens when you try to get better?

Since we are here in this incredibly complicated world of pain, is it still perhaps useful to meditate, as long as one does it in the proper context, that is, as a means of cultivating the space between thoughts where clinging to pain can end? Otherwise, all one has is an intellectual grasp of the truth, an approximation, that can never heal one completely. In the midst of illness and depression, one can hardly hope to be spontaneously visited by the collapse of the web of self, can one? This would smack too much of the Christian concept of grace.

In other words, "All right, I get it, there is nothing one can do. But now, what do I do with that?" Shift the perspective of what our spirituality is about. The "doing" that we have all been involved in has been solution-oriented—finding resolution, enlightenment, peace, etc. What if we truly give up on all that, even the cultivation of spaciousness? What is meditation, then? Are we still drawn to it, and if so, what is it? The very investigation of this quality of "being without doing" and "doing without a doer" is the meditation. It is going on all the time, whether we're sitting in formal meditation or doing anything else.

The web of the self is already collapsed. We already live in grace.

I still don't understand how embracing your very lucid proposal leads to the cessation of pain in a doubting mind. Isn't it just as reasonable to conclude that life's a bitch and then you die?

I'm not suggesting that the cessation of pain is a particular goal, or that life isn't a bitch. And regardless of any of this, it certainly looks like we will die. I am asking whether it is possible for us to organize our reality around something other than the conceptual "me," and if so, what would that be? This is an open-ended question, rather than a conclusion.

I guess if we were permanently free of unhappiness, there would be no need for any search or inquiry. I remember the freedom I felt when I was younger, quitting a job just because I was fed up with it. Now like most, I cling to the mortgage, business, car. There is little hope of being free of unhappiness while we cling to these structures through fear of loss of comfort, love, or prestige. But surely we see the identification with the mind or self as it creeps into a young child, as the conditioning takes over. Is it not about shedding the excess baggage while retaining the practical lessons of living? I guess then, we need to take practical steps, rather than anything spiritual, to rid ourselves of unhappiness.

We cling to our structures because we believe they will give us security, but we still feel agitation because we know that things don't actually make us secure. Total security comes from a radically different relationship to our thought world, which occurs naturally and spontaneously in the timelessness of each moment.

I doubt we are going to be very successful at shedding anything, except perhaps the idea that we should be successful at shedding our baggage. It also seems entirely imaginary that there is a state that is permanently happy, other than one that results from a major brain injury. What if our baggage is just there, as it is?

Life is change. Nothing is permanent—happiness or unhappiness—and giving up the attempt to make any particular state permanent is as direct and available as just being still.

Empathy and Social Action

How do you see the discoveries of quantum physics changing how we are with each other?

In the middle of the 20th Century, John Bell outlined a logical limitation to the influence that particles had on each other if the classic physical description of reality was accurate. He showed, in what was to become known as Bell's Theorem, that the influence these separated particles had on each other was actually far greater than classic physics allowed, and thus he questioned the very nature of separability. Supporting experiments proved that there are unexplained influences between particles even at vast distances, influences operating faster than the speed of light. That is, they are outside of what science recognizes as cause and effect.

The implications of Bell's Theorem are not completely understood by physicists, who are debating to this day what this tells us about the nature of reality. Our world appears to be interconnected by forces that, in their instantaneousness, make it difficult to see any true and complete separation. Quantum physics is telling us the same thing the mystics have always told us. Although the scientist is not yet allowed to say it, the mystic can. We are one.

So if I come into contact with someone in need, I can walk by and pretend I don't see him, but the fact is that person and I are in relation to one another on a fundamental particulate level. I could say, "Well I don't need to do anything about this person," but in fact I need to have some response for myself. This is the molecular basis of empathy. Somewhere we understand that we are the same. Something that touches you, touches me. Someone who is dying of starvation in Africa is somewhere in me. This is why it's so important to find out what we really are.

So if enough people recognize that we are interdependent, then the person in Africa won't die of starvation, because we'll see to it that there's an equitable distribution of food.

But it's not just that the person in Africa won't die. It's that I won't die as a human being. It's my own poverty, my own disconnection. We don't generally die here from lack of food. We die from lack of empathy, lack of love.

If you're operating within the framework of time, then I'm separate from the man who is dying in Africa. But when we actually experience the Bell's theorem of the heart—which is that your pain is in fact not in the other, it's in me—then there's no time. Now there's no one to be saved, there's just something in me to be understood. There's the need to understand why I'm starving.

I predicated my life for a while on the notion that we invented time to learn how to direct change. The idea was that we could change the fulcrum of the duality balance, so that evil would fall away forever. I would hate to give that up to dwell in silence.

Let me make it clear that I'm not equating silence with nihilism or inaction. We have a spiritual image that silence means we stop doing, and sit in a dark, sealed-off cave. Not at all. Silence occurs when the conceptual framework, which keeps us divided, becomes transparent. In that moment, there is action.

Without silence, when we meet someone in need, we have the clutter of judgment and ideas, so there's no direct action. We can't even see who's in front of us. We can't feel that the person is actually inside us, so we don't know what action to take. Sometimes the action is to walk by, sometimes it's to give, sometimes it's to bring the person into your home. But we can't know that, because we're so cluttered. This is a world in which we're all actors, because we're all responsible.

How do you unclutter?

Let's start with where we are, which is that we are cluttered. We inhabit a world of thoughts, coming and going. There's a macro-thought wrapping around all the other thoughts. That macro-thought tells us, "I am. These are my thoughts. This is my life."

What do I do about that? What the actor, the doer, says I should do about it is the same thing as the thoughts themselves. Whatever my conditioning is, that's what I should do about it. So thought replicates itself. I'm suggesting that in the face of that, you don't do anything. Doing nothing is not about concrete action. It's about psychological action, about how we relate to our own mind structures. The very position of not doing is a powerful response, but it's difficult for us to ideate what that means. This approach is a negative response, rather than to do something.

Let's take the energy out of the whole mental framework and let it be where it is, which is in awareness, the backdrop. Then let's see what arises out of that. If I were to try to describe what that is, the description would become another concept. Once we understand what the clutter is, then the inquiry becomes, "What is expressing out of wholeness?" You can't find division in awareness; its expression is whole.

Children and Community

How does the principle of "doing nothing" work in life?

We believe that it can't work, and that the known hell of the world we have collectively created is at least known. The answer to the question, "How do we engage in a life that is committed to freedom from conflict?" is unknown. The unknown generates fear simply because it is unknown. It requires relationship, and commitment to the cutting edge of our own understanding.

The life of exploration is actualized when we have no other choice, when the life we are living doesn't work anymore. I will assert to you (but you will have to find this to be true or untrue in your own life) that life will always respond when we move not from conflict but from relatedness. This is not feel-good spirituality. It is the fact of full-contact living, inspired not by self-preservation, but by full communion with each other and with life itself.

Jesus says that the love of money is the root of all evil. Ramakrishna says that women and gold are the ruination of man. I'm aware that they are talking about greed and lust. But I don't think one can simply shun greed and lust. I think money should be viewed realistically for what it is, congealed energy. Money can be liquid love, when used properly. If money is hoarded for the power it seems to represent, then it becomes toxic. As for women, my wife has made me a more complete, humane being and she feels I have done the same for her.

The shunning of money and women is about the same as the addiction to them. Greed and lust are certainly two of the strongest drives. Survival and reproduction are no doubt wired into our biology as well as conditioned in our psychological structures. What is more to the point is an intelligent relationship to the world around us, including money and the intimate relationships we have.

It would be much easier if there were just something to join, some group or whatever. But there's not.

There is the relatedness that is in every life, and the forms of expression of that are myriad. Often I find that a cynicism grows within us with age: "Something should have happened and it hasn't, so it never will." Instead of this cynicism, we could be opening to the current possibilities of relationship and the forms it expresses. It's not "How do I fix myself?" but "What is the expression of relatedness?"

I find that community is in the immediate contact I have with those I meet, and in a more concrete sense, with those who choose to coordinate their lives or work with me. In my own expression I travel a lot and talk with people in formal and informal settings, as well as write books. But for each of us there seems to be an expression if we embrace the fact of interrelatedness.

Go for the relatedness, if that's really what you want. Follow that instinct, which is not the aversion to loneliness, or the reaction to a misconstructed life, or running from problems with current relationships and responsibilities, but the deep need for honest and open contact. This is not withheld from any of us, other than by the veil of our own deluded concepts about our personal security and our fear.

But what does "relatedness" mean?

We generally sort our experiences into what we want and don't want, and on a macro level we do the same with the people in our lives, the circumstances, etc. What if we stop sorting and open up to all of it? What if we begin to construct the forms in our lives—family, work, community, schools, etc.—not around security and survival but around connection and communication? Relatedness is the fact of our life—the fact that we are inextricably imbedded in each other, and really in everything. Living in relatedness has more to do with letting go of the concepts that divide us, than it does with doing something about relatedness. We have a very short time in form, just a moment. What will we give expression to? This shared inquiry is the movement of relatedness.

Please give me some guidance. I am a 45-year-old married man, deeply committed to my spiritual life. I've got a problem I can't resolve. As the years go by, I find myself more attracted to the youthful beauty of women in their twenties.

If we are truly committed to a spiritual life, then we must also be committed to honesty, wherever it takes us. A relationship to another human being is a tremendous opportunity for discovery, but it can also be used to avoid contact with the rest of life.

Most relationships are built on mutual security: "I'll love you, if you love me." They become complex codes of behavior in which we tend to lose the essence of our contact with each other. Then along comes a lovely young woman or man, vital, fresh, not encumbered by the labyrinth of behavioral codes we have built up over the years with our spouse.

We want this fresh quality, we want the youth, we want the sex. We could have a secret affair. We could divorce and remarry. Or, we could repress our feelings and live the resulting quiet desperation of an unfulfilled life. But, none of these responses are satisfactory.

Why don't we stand absolutely still in the middle of all this and discover what is actually occurring? What happens if we don't act or repress? Why don't we reveal all that is happening in our lives to all of those in our lives? This is a radically direct relationship to ourselves, our spouses, and to the object of our new attraction, which demands total integrity and communication.

Is our current relationship based in honesty and spiritual transformation? Can our current relationship absorb the fact that we are experiencing attractions to others? Do we live in a relationship of freedom, responsibility, and transparency with each other, or do we have a treaty based on security? If we throw out all our agreements, is there love? Is there fear? If we meet each other now, as if for the first time, how would we construct our relationship and why?

And how would we enter into an honest relationship with a new person to whom we find ourselves attracted? Would we encounter this new person in a new way or would we again begin to construct agreements of security? Would we flirt by hiding our flaws? Would we court by hiding our wife or husband? What happens to the magical charge of the new relationship if it is openly exposed to the old relationship? What if the whole game is made transparent? Do we still want to play the game?

My response to your question is this. Honesty will challenge your marriage. Honesty may deepen your marriage. Honesty may destroy your marriage. But, honesty will reveal precisely the fact of your life. This honesty applies not just to your communication with others, where the idea of radical honesty often becomes a narcissistic way of dominating others. Honesty must also apply to your understanding of your own motivations and ultimately to the very nature of the construction of your self as separate from life. In the end, transformation is the movement of change in life. Honesty is just the messenger.

You suggest that our work "should be an extension of our silence," but with all the economic pressures in today's world how can one earn enough money to lead a reasonably comfortable life, freeing up time for this inquiry?

We each have the capacity to generate a life unburdened by financial pressures. The interplay of fear and insecurity along with the need for identity, purpose, and defining activity leave most people driving forward on an endless treadmill. Anyone can penetrate the mind structures, which are essentially survival oriented, and open to the actual movement of consciousness, which is essentially secure and whole. This answers the financial question.

The money question, after all, is simply a metaphor for our chances of survival. We need more money to assure our security, and that carrot-on-the-stick keeps us running through our life. But the money metaphor misses the point of life entirely, which is that life is symbiotic, not individual. Deep in each of us is the passion to live that fact of relatedness, but fear instructs us to take care of our security first, and we are paralyzed.

We have it backwards. Living from the drive for security expresses itself as what it is—insecurity and lack. Living from the passion of relatedness expresses itself as what it is—love and security, including financial. The pathways to financial prosperity are present in each of our lives already, as quantum potential, but like Kabir's thirsty fish, we do not recognize it.

Holistic prosperity is not wealth per se, but "just enough" for the individual, and the excess is given over to the related world around. For some this may be a very simple material life, for others who may be good at the generation of wealth, this may mean a philanthropic life. The essential element is not the quantity of wealth, but rather the full embrace of life. This is where happiness lies.

The mechanics of holistic prosperity are straightforward. Perceive the need for security as the ground to your life's work, not as the end, but as an integral part of any life expression. Dedicate the excess that you may accumulate to those in need.

Integrate your expression. Let go of the mask and let your face show. Commune with those who share your vision. Communicate with those who don't. Your life is interactive, informing and being informed.

Cooperate in the logistics of life. A living community is the greatest wealth builder. Share the business, house, kitchen, and car. Tremendous resources are wasted on the lonely lives encapsulated in the suburban house and urban apartment.

Unleash the passion of purpose in yourself, regardless of how it fits in your current life. You may or may not lose friends, colleagues, your spouse, or the approval of society. Trust the flow of your passion. It isn't rational, but it can use the rational mind as a tool and a technology to make things work. It isn't emotional, although it deeply feels the flow of emotions as vital information about relationship. It is the integral viewpoint, which puts together the individual as actor and the whole as context, in each moment.

Remember, it's about transformational living. The passion thing, the money thing, the what do I do with my life thing—all these are subsumed by the mystical fact of the energy of consciousness moving through our lives.

You know what *not* jumping off the cliff is, but you can't know what jumping off the cliff is without jumping. Nobody can tell you how to do it. Nobody can do it for you. Living our passion is not dangerous. It is much worse. It is unknown. But what is known can never be new or creative. If we die in our passion, at least we have lived. If we live in the known, we have already died.

Why are you interested in intentional, residential community?

Interesting things happen when we put ourselves in a living situation where the challenges of life are met with the same inquiry and transparency that we usually create only in the rarified atmosphere of a public dialogue or weekend retreat. What kind of community will we structure out of this intensity to live fully? Can this be brought into the practicality of our lives, or is it just some abstract verbiage? Further, for those of us who are raising children, there is a great need for safe, creative, stable, and loving environments.

So perhaps the question is, can parallel lives converge?

To answer this question, go to a very long and straight section of railroad track.

Look down the track. What was parallel appears to converge.

Notice a large object hurtling towards you? Get out of the way. Quickly. This is another possible means of convergence, but it is very messy.

Why do you have children? Doing nothing and not identifying with the doer takes intense focus, so why would you take on a relationship that distracts you from that inner focus?

It takes tremendous energy to maintain separation. Wholeness is effortless. Children aren't distractions from life. They are life's expressions.

But children require you to take responsibility for them. If we act in response to the external circumstances, instead of in response to the internal movement, aren't we caught in form? Doesn't the wholeness of reality flow only from formlessness?

What are the rules you have set up for yourself as to how life works? The problem with non-duality as a philosophy is that it becomes a set of ideas that we then compare to our actuality. The actuality is the fact of our life, and perhaps that includes noisy, demanding children who take us away from what we thought were our priorities. But we now discover, through these children, that these priorities were simply a concept. Is it possible that formlessness, form, and wholeness are all a singularity?

I participated in a recent group dialogue with you and did not get much out of the experience. I was expecting something entirely different from what occurred. Of course, I didn't really do much to influence the direction of things myself.

It seemed clear to me you are looking to develop serious relationships with others, which might lead to a higher level of community. My sense is, as we come to a more direct reflection of experience in our relationships, a very different way of being comes into view. I have experimented with this on a very small scale with others, holding our exchange to our direct experience, allowing a somewhat expanded sense of "presence" to orient or at least influence speech, feeling, thought, etc. I cannot think of another experience with others I found so significant.

The quality of the group dialogue was a reflection of the people in the room and the state of the human being. Any expectations I might have are irrelevant.

Your experience of the event as unsatisfactory may well have been shared by everyone, but each was unwilling to challenge the others. Or perhaps these are people caught up in their reasoning minds, while you are ready for something different. It is difficult to know with certainty what did occur in that room, although we can easily know our interpretation of what occurred.

Each person in that room, or anywhere else for that matter, can demand a deep and fundamental relationship with each other. And each person can remain in the illusion of separation. I was invited to come there, and I did. I expressed what was present and responded to what was there. There was very little to draw anyone to that room or to keep them there. Perhaps you could construct an event that reflects the qualities you are looking for or are interested in, and follow that experiment.

I am interested in a life that reflects the qualities of my perception. I am literally inviting the world to join in this inquiry, this experiment, through my books and talks. But I have no interest in convincing anyone to join me. The integrity of my life is the willingness to stand alone in that perception. Those who have no choice but to join in will. Those who have any other choice whatsoever will not.

Do you know of any group of people who are expressing the mystic realization of oneness with all life? Is anyone building a society based on this realization? Is the capacity to live a life of love needed in the world?

There is just this relationship—you and me—and each that is touched by this relationship, which is all and everything. There is just this life as it is. The integration of the mystic realization with the mundane is the challenge of life.

I have found a deep need to explore the qualities of this existence, to communicate with those I contact, and to be of some help to those whose needs are obvious. The structures of my life, my relationships, and my "society" have grown from this expression.

Perhaps we can build a culture that reflects the mystic realization, but first can we live it ourselves? Can you and I live it in our relationship? If so, then we have the new society. If not, then there is a different question that brings us in contact with what we are and how we are. This actuality is what we have to work with, to discover within, and to transform.

You ask whether this capacity of love is needed somewhere. Of course, it is needed everywhere. You and I must express it everywhere by expressing it here.

I feel good about my creativity, yet somehow I feel bad because I enjoy the recognition I receive for it. How does "doing nothing" fit here?

The feeling of pleasure and then the guilt of pleasure (and perhaps at some point, the feeling of pleasure at having understood the guilt of pleasure, and then the guilt of that pleasure) start to look like a cycle—not two things, but one. This one cycle—a kind of agitation of being—requires the energy of our involvement (trying to fix it, change it, etc.) to sustain it. Non-involvement leaves the cycle as it is. We feel pleasure. We feel guilt. And then we feel what is next.

I have somewhat half-heartedly started a religious education for my oldest child, mostly because I did not know what else to do. She is a bright child and, of course, sees right through my ambivalence. I want to simply be truthful and tell her how I feel and yet I am afraid to do that, in part because I do not want to remove the security blanket of belief that must be very comforting for a child.

I have a great trust in the capacity of a child to express what the child actually needs to a parent who is willing to listen. The gift we can give our children is to listen and respond in an open, honest way. The catastrophe for me would not be what life delivers, but the beliefs we impose on our kids out of our own fears, which is an attempt to limit them to what we already know is not true. This is essentially a narcissistic act and an avoidance of our own inner work.

It seems from what you have said that you already know all this but don't know what to do about it. Not knowing is a tremendously dynamic point, one worth exploring and sharing with your children, as it is the heart of mysticism, the driving force of creativity, and the essence of a child's innate nature.

How do we bring this kind of spirituality to our children?

It is unnecessary to condition any child with ideas of spirituality, but we can infuse our lives with this inquiry in everything we are and do. Explore what this means in terms of family structure, intentional community, creative school environment, and all the structures of our world.

In relation to your work and in observing children, what have you understood about the development of personality, ego, conditioning, and habits?

Biology seems to unfold specific cognitive and developmental stages. Sometimes it looks like biology—the imbedded memory of the genes and cells—is the director, and it is a fantasy that anything else is running the show. It can look a lot like the sociobiologist's view that the body exists for the delivery of the genetic matter to the next generation, and not a lot more. There is a whole different exploration, which is about the inherent relationship you discover with particular individuals in your life. Why did a particular meeting take place, go deep, and touch such love? Why isn't every relationship like this? Why do we have the capacity to love each other and yet we don't?

There is so much of the conditioned past imbedded in the parent/child relationship. Perhaps this is why the relationship is often strained. How do we heal and enhance these relationships?

Drop the idea of parent and child when it no longer applies. Parents control their children as if that was parenting. We have a function to care for and protect the child, not condition the child to respond to us in a particular way. Education is not indoctrination; it is freedom to pursue what interests a child. Rebellion grows from the perception of hypocrisy. Responsibility is natural to a child, if the child is given choices and understands the consequences for himself and the impact on those around him. To me the healing and the enhancement of any relationship is to recognize the bare actuality of what it is and what we are in the relationship. The resistance to this actuality, and the conceptual fog that is the expression of that resistance, is the conflict.

How do you suggest we relate to our wives or husbands within the historical male/female roles? What happens to these roles if we examine our lives with the intensity you are suggesting?

Let's relate to each other as we are, not as a role, as a male or a female, as a wife or husband. Why is it necessary to have this kind of patterned behavior? We have seen that it doesn't work. What if a relationship is not designed to exclude the rest of the world, and we interact vigorously with anyone who is interested? If we are interested in relationship with the whole, we cannot then be entirely defined by a marriage or a nuclear family, or even an extended family, a community, or any variation of grouping. I am interested in relationship—total relationship—with each person I meet.

What happens when we look at our relationships with intensity? We lose the security of the known pattern. This inherent insecurity in the relationship, this freedom of expression, is the only hope for any relationship.

Many of the writers in the fields of spirituality and transpersonal psychology these days are saying that ego is a necessary stage in the evolution of consciousness and that it is a step on the journey towards enlightenment. In other words, being an ego is just something you have to go through. How do you feel about that?

There is a clear biological and developmental task that the human organism must go through, which can be observed in children. If you want to describe that process conceptually and then reify that conceptual description by calling it ego development, you can do that. But it seems far more basic to me than that.

The biological organism needs to learn to function in the world. In order to accomplish that, it becomes experimental. Part of that experiment is to figure out if it is better to take or to give. Taking works, at least at a certain age. For example, a four-year-old takes things from a two-year-old and it works, in that he gets the toy. That's one way we learn, but there's also a more subtle learning taking place. When he takes from the other, he gets the object, but he loses the relationship. You can see in him the beginning of an observation, "Okay, I've got the toy, but I don't have the playmate." And without the playmate, the toy is no fun. Soon, the child learns to share in order to have the relationship. So, is it natural that we are egotistical, or is it natural that we're connected? Empathy is actually biologically intelligent.

Let me restate the question. Is it inevitable that children grow up and develop a sense of self, a sense of ego?

The self as a biological fact is not the problem. Kids need to know the difference between their body and the dog down the street that bites. That's basic intelligence. But with that comes a kind of integral intelligence, which has to do with the relationship function. That is also biological. It's not abstracted at all. We need each other to survive.

But it goes deeper than that, doesn't it? We are one another. It's not just about survival.

And that is true biologically as well. We're not actually a species. The world isn't divided up into humans and animals and plants. Those are just conceptual categories. There is actually an intermingling of life on all levels, a great symbiosis of life forms expressing as Gaia, a world interconnected and alive.

Let's assume that we are able to create a structure in our lifetime that is truly egalitarian and actuality-based, like your alternative school idea, or the living community. And then you die. What happens? Entropy sets in, and what you created for one reason ends up metamorphosing into something else.

Life is expressing itself through each of us. Life will discard my body when it's not needed anymore. Perhaps in the next moment. It *will* be the next moment because the next moment is all there is.

So, this body will expire. That's just fine, because life has the intelligence. Intelligence does not originate with this body; it's in the *whole* of life. In that respect, the movement of life through my body, your body, our children, our family, our friends, is all the same life.

I'm not concerned about what happens after I die. The whole is the whole. This is simply the undulation of life. It has its own pattern and force.

What's So

Is there a better way to understand what's being said? I hear these words, and I can't quite hang on to them. Is there a better way to communicate what you're trying to communicate?

Mostly what happens is that people think, "Well these words are confusing. I need words that don't confuse me." Then they go to the next set of words, and then the next set of words. Eventually they look back on their life and say that it was all meaningless, because it was full of word meaning.

The access point is to stand still, realize you are in a relationship, and find what expresses in that stillness. What do you actually experience in your entire perceptual field? What is aware of the entire perceptual field? That deep silence, which is energetic and dynamic in nature, is what is actually happening in this room. The words are just what we do because we're speaking animals.

If you listen to the words and try to make sense of them, all you're going to do is either agree or disagree. If you agree, you'll like it. If you disagree, you won't like it. You're just in the realm of like and dislike.

I feel that I am most with people when there are very few words, and a lot of silence. It would be wonderful, even in this room, to be with each other in silence.

We can create this room in a way that you would fall silent just by walking into it. The people who do that are the most popular, most powerful teachers, because they know how to set it up. They have their core group, the flowers, the stage. Some of them have signs that say "Please be Quiet" when you come in. So we can stage it to create silence and the feeling of immensity.

I'm not afraid of words. Words hold technological information. We could be singing, dancing, drawing. That wouldn't hold totality either.

I think that music does hold those qualities.

Does the sound hold the space, or does the space hold the sound?

The space holds the sound.

That's all I'm saying. You don't get to the space through the words. The space can flow through the words, or the song, or the dance, or the silence.

It doesn't make any difference. Techniques such as music, dance, art, and language are the expression of wholeness. You are an expression of wholeness. The idea that there is something separate that can be strengthened or weakened by our choosing certain actions is the illusion. Choice, the separate ego, and the strengthening or weakening of it, are all just ideas, illusions. You are animated by wholeness. That's it. Now see how long you can just be with that before the voice comes in and says, "Yes, but when I do this thing it hurts, therefore I have to correct it." The voice is insubstantial. It's empty.

It compounds itself because it's happening so rapidly. We're so used to talking to ourselves, essentially. Talking about ourselves to ourselves. It's happening so quickly that it looks substantial. But if life is animating you, then the game's over. Live!

Now what will you do with your life? What if it's not about fixing yourself, or correcting yourself, or surviving, or accumulating wealth or power or control, whether within your marriage or your family or your society? It's not about any of those things. You are an expression of life. Then what is it about?

Nothing.

Is it nothing or is it everything?

Both.

Now you have the inquiry, the investigation of that dynamic expression. That's what your life is now; it's the expression of that inquiry. That's what we're doing here, today, now. I'm not here to fix myself. I'm not here to fix you. I know I can't be helpful to you in any way. I can't help myself in any way. So, begin to investigate the expression of wholeness.

We have discovered, just now, that we are here. We are in the moment. We are the expression of life.

So we've discovered that. What now?

What is "now"? What are you finding in this moment?

Joy.

Some moments from now, you'll leave this room, and you'll go into the rest of your life.

It leaves me in a place where I just don't know.

We came in not knowing and that's how we're going to leave.

We don't have the clear voice of God saying, "Do this now." What we have is the voice of the moment; it is very clear. It's not a voice in words, it's not a voice in song, it's not a voice in art. It's a voice in life.

It's the voice of stillness or silence. It is clear in this moment. When we look back at our life to predict what to do next, and we find the chaos and meaningless of our past, we try to apply that to the future. That's when we begin to say, "What should we do? What is life about?" But in this moment, it's clear.

Thought occurs in a moment, but thought can't interpret the moment. Thought can interpret only a series of moments that it can capture conceptually and call "time." Then, now, and about to be—that's time, that's thought.

Clarity resides in the moment because the nature of the moment is that it's free of time, it's free of thought.

Thought is really in the past or future.

Thought takes place in a subject/object world, so there's a past referred to from now, or a past taken into the future as a prediction.

In the moment you really can't conceptualize it.

Thought takes place in a moment, and concept can be used in a moment, but the moment is not bounded by thought because it's timeless.

Why is that better than living in a conceptual world? So what?

It's not that it is better. It's where we are. We are in the moment, and the conceptual world only posits that we're not. I'm not trying to get at "better"; I'm only trying to get at what is. Because I've noticed that when I'm relating in my conceptual world, I'm not relating to anything. I'm relating to something that is insubstantial and yet appears to be real.

If I can never actually have a relationship to you, I am driven to understand why that is. As I look into it, I find that the failure of relationship exists only when I extrapolate this moment into many moments. That abstracted world isn't really findable. It's not anywhere.

What I can find is this moment. It's never inaccessible, it's never far away, and I don't need anybody to show it to me, nor do you. It's not a profound, big deal. It's just that finally, I can discover where I am.

It's what's so.

And from what's so, I can begin to discover the world in a very different way. Not as a child, because I'm no longer a child. I'm able to organize the world conceptually. But I'm no longer bound by the conceptual world, because I understand its function and limitation.

In the moment there's no history. There's no future to worry about. There's a very dynamic state. It's the moment of quantum potential. Anything can happen in this moment.

Discovering the Dynamic Question

When we try to determine the nature of life, we must start with the deep understanding that we have no understanding. This is perhaps the most profound knowledge that we can come to in life. It means that we recognize something about the way thought operates. Thought captures some, but not all, of life. We have put so much time, energy, and culture into thought, which scoops out just a little bit of life but describes that little bit as if that were the whole of life.

Our movement through life is based on concepts. We create our relationships, families, communities, and other social structures around our thoughts. Our thoughts appear to us to be substantial and whole, the entirety of life. But perhaps at some point a crack occurs—there is a death, an illness, or a tragedy. Perhaps it just occurs spontaneously. But in that crack in the conceptual reality, something else emerges.

It is the breakdown of our life. We might call it chaos or insanity, or perhaps it is characterized as something spiritual. We quickly try to find someone who can explain what is happening. If it is a psychologist, then we get a psychological explanation. If it is a spiritual teacher, we get a spiritual explanation. And if we find nobody to explain the breakdown of our conceptual world, then perhaps we become disoriented, disassociated, and disconnected.

What emerges from the breakdown of the conceptual world is nothing more than a question. It's not an answer. It's not anything that can be captured by any of the systems of philosophy, or spirituality, or religion. It is actually the movement of life itself, which is always changing, always moving, always dynamic. It can't be captured by the conceptual world because it's not entirely in that realm.

We've come to the point where we don't know. We've come to this point without any explanation for not knowing. We're not crazy. We're not spiritual. We just don't know. It's very comforting to be crazy or spiritual, but there's something uncomfortable about not knowing. No concept, answer, or form holds the unknown. Yet the obvious fact, when you stop and stand still in your life, is that we exist *in* the unknown *as* the unknown. There is no action that we can take from the known or from our concepts that doesn't create more of the same. There's no way out of the conceptual world through the conceptual world. There is only the abrupt and sudden cessation of that world as our guide.

Something about the unknown is moving into and through the conceptual world. It's moving into the relationships that we have created. Rather than trying to get to consciousness or get to the unknown, we can ask what the unknown wants with us. What is the unknown infusing into my relationship with my child, my spouse, my boss? We can discover what that means in relationship to each of the people in our lives. Is there anything that we can do together? Can we join together in this exploration?

There's no answer to that. Do we have the capacity to actually stand in the silence of no answer? Can we live in that? Not as a state, not as something that feels good or bad, but just as the fact that we don't know.

I find it very disturbing to think that there's just a void and we don't know what it's all about. I think that the reason we're here is to experience the physical world and become better spirits.

Well, try that. See if that explanation works any better than the last hundred explanations you've tried out. We're taking one explanation and living through that, finding out that it doesn't work, taking on the next one, living through that, and so on.

But there's got to be some anchor, something to grasp.

Find out if that's true. Do we need an anchor? The way that thought is structured, it appears that we need an anchor. The anchor is called "me." I need "me" so I'll know what to do. But this anchor works in a way that separates by its nature and is destructive in its expression. The anchor of "me" means that I have to be dominant over you. That's the nature of it. It puts me in a competitive relationship.

Why is it competitive?

When I look at you, I see you outside of myself, and I see myself centered here. I know that there are only certain resources available. Perhaps I'm bigger than you or I can get to those resources faster. I may be smarter or richer. Thought is a mechanism by which to assess the environment and understand how to survive in it.

When I speak to people, such as this group, thought assesses this environment and sees a lot of people I don't know. Those people are threats. It sees a few people I do know. Those people are problems. In thought, the only thing that I can be certain about is that I'm here, located in this "me," and I know where the door is. Thought constantly assesses the environment so that I will survive.

Can you stop doing that, if you want to?

Well, I've tried to stop doing that. I went to my psychologist and I practiced stopping there. I examined my childhood and I got rebirthed. I went to my meditation teacher. I got my mantra. I tried so many things. Drugs, alcohol, hitting my head against the wall. And still I was assessing the environment to find out in subtle and complex ways how to survive. How can I survive physically? How do I get food, resources, clothes, and shelter? How do I survive psychologically? How do I become prominent? How do I become famous? How do I become rich? How do I become important, respected, intelligent?

That's a world of constant assessment and prediction based on the model of the past, which allows me to go through the future in the same way I went through the past. I survived the past, therefore I will survive the future, provided I keep the same habits going. The whole world of thought and conceptualization is built around the survival of "me." This means not just the survival of my body, but also the psychological self—this bundle of ideas about myself that you threaten. If you don't love me and say good things about me, then right now you could trash me in front of all these people. I have to be really wary of you.

It's pretty scary.

Right, we're terrified. That's what we're doing with each other all the time. That's the world that is generated from "me." It can't fully embody the world of "us." It can try to do it philosophically, politically, or spiritually, but attached to that conceptualization is the sense of survival.

I still believe that there has to be a way to let go, to allow inclusion and acceptance.

There is no "way." Can you demonstrate the technology that creates instant enlightenment? The collective experience so far seems to be that the pursuit of such technologies leaves us pursuing the technologies. The attempt to meditate, to practice, to get something always leaves us pushing forward, so that we never actually rest where we are. What if it's not about letting go? What if we do nothing about the fact that we're holding on?

Doing nothing is a process, too.

How is it a process?

There's a momentary relief, and then I'm back to the cycle of thoughts.

What if you don't create the idea of letting go? What happens? What if you don't do even that? What if you don't modify the sense of contraction that's taking place before you let go?

I find myself climbing a wall with grease on it. I don't get anywhere.

And what if you keep doing that?

I get tired.

What if you continue to not get anywhere instead of creating the cycle of contraction and release? You feel contracted, you feel that you're not getting anywhere, so you create the idea of letting go. You find the expansion that you've learned how to get to, and experience a feeling of release. What if you don't do that? What if you don't go through the cycles of up and down?

Sometimes you give up.

What if you just stayed "given up"? Not as an idea, but facing the fact that all these attempts just create the opposite. Facing the fact that the idea of release just creates a sense of release, which eventually contracts and creates the need for the release again. Isn't the problem the whole business of going through the cycle—the addiction to release, the fear of contraction?

We're so conditioned to that. We are constantly trying to solve problems.

We've been conditioned to that through all our spirituality. What if we don't continue with our spirituality?

What is the purpose of being spiritual? You might as well quit that, too.

Look at what happens when you consider quitting the spiritual path. Look at the fear. Who am I if I'm not spiritual? What will I do if I'm not spiritual? There we are. There's the unknown.

Will quitting bring you joy?

The whole of life is not just joy. It's also the problems. The trouble with following joy is that we're trying to get away from everything sad. We won't discover joy by chasing it. Trying to maintain joy as a permanent condition is a formula for pain.

Doing nothing would apply very well to that. If you're happy, okay, but don't try to pursue happiness. If you're sad the next minute, that's fine, because it all comes around sometime or other. Don't force it one way or the other.

I now have the ideal that I shouldn't be doing anything about anything. So now I think, "I'm going to take on happiness or sadness and everything's going to be fine because I'm going to do nothing." Then I start to find that there's a pressure in me to do nothing, and what I really want is to do something. I'm feeling sad, I'm feeling like I'm climbing the wall. It's greased, so I'm not getting anywhere and I want to let go, but no, I'm supposed to do nothing.

You're asking the impossible, I'm afraid.

I'm not asking anything of you. You don't have to do anything about any of this. I'm just asking if we can see what we're doing. Each of us is constantly trying to create a concept, thought, technology, or way of living that creates a permanent state of safety for our self. I'm not trying to create a state in which *we* are safe, in which all of life is safe. That's not it at all. I'm trying to create a state in which *I* am safe.

So I've tried all these things and none of them have worked, and now I hear about doing nothing. That sounds like a good idea. I'll do nothing, and that will make me safe. Now when I feel sad, I'll do nothing. But then I find that when I feel sad, there's something arising in me that wants to feel better. Well, I shouldn't do that. I should do nothing. The neurotic mind has come back, and is trying to create this divided universe in which I'm not doing enough of nothing.

It seems to me that you would just sit there and not be motivated to move in any direction. There's no reason to get up or sit down.

I no longer energize any motivation coming from me. That is, when a thought comes up to do something, or to do nothing, in order to survive, no energy goes into that at all.

Even beyond survival, it seems to me there's no motivation to do anything for any reason.

Does something move from life itself that motivates us? Are we animated by life, or are we animated by this neurotic drive for survival? The only way we can discover that is by looking at the survival drive clearly.

Perhaps that leaves us sitting here empty, without motion or motivation. We would die. And that's actually what we have to do. We have to die psychologically. The psychological self says, "I don't want to die; I need to survive. I can find a way to be okay."

There is no way to be okay, because the field of thought is inherently divided. Every thought has a subject/object relationship to the world around it. Every thought divides the world. There's no thought that is whole. Because it's a divided world, there's always something outside of me that is a threat. That world of thought can never be stable. We can meditate for a thousand years and thought will still be divided. It will still have a subject and an object.

Go to the place in yourself in which nothing energizes your personal thought, your personal world. There you can face the death to the personal.

What about your subconscious? You can think all you want, but your subconscious is going to pursue survival regardless of what you try to do or not do.

I don't care what the mind generates: subconscious, conscious, or superconscious. I understand that anything the mind comes up with is of the conceptual world, which is based on my survival. The pain of that is more than I can bear anymore. I have totally given up trying to do anything about it. Is there anything else, or is it just a world of thought in which we're battling with each other for our personal survival, making alliances, making relationships based on "I'm okay, you're okay, aren't we?"

Is it possible to think of doing nothing outside the conceptual world? We are innately driven to do things rationally or conceptually, and you're asking us to step beyond that.

Try to think about doing nothing. What is it?

That process of thought takes me right to where I started. I haven't gone anywhere.

And you won't go anywhere. Anything that's spoken or written can become a concept. So, discard "doing nothing." It's just a phrase, designed to turn the mind on itself, into silence.

Are you saying to jettison all thought and you have reality?

It's hopeless to try to get rid of thought. You don't have to do anything with thought. We have the idea that because we think, we therefore have to act. We believe we have to relate to thought as if thought is the totality.

We sort thoughts into those that make us feel good and those that make us feel bad, and then we try to keep the bad ones out. A lot of our psychological world involves trying to sustain the thoughts that cause oceanic feelings and get rid of the thoughts that make us feel fearful and anxious. We think if we just stay in one part of our brain, we'll be okay.

All we really have to do is understand what thought is, and let thought do what it's doing, which it will anyway. In that apprehending of what thought is, is something else occurring? Is something else occurring right now, which we're not noticing because we're so embedded in the world as thought?

Sociologically, maybe part of the problem is our highly individualistic culture. We have more of a sense of "I" than exists in some other cultures. In some cultures, people define themselves by their relationship to their family or a larger group.

Communism structures resources differently than capitalism. Tribal culture is different from suburban culture in the ways it structures people's relationships to each other. Those are modifications, but there's still no expression in concept for a holistic relationship.

"Holistic" means not disregarding the individual or the whole, but integrating them. The fact is that I do have a body that needs to be fed. Feeding the village while disregarding this body doesn't allow this body to survive. Somehow we must have a capacity that takes in and integrates everything. If we have that capacity, where does it reside?

It does not reside in thought. It's just not there. Let's see what else there is. Thought tells us, "Don't leave me, don't go away, don't withdraw your energy from me, because you'll die. I am your protector. If you don't think about everything, then you won't survive."

I'm interested in finding out if there's anything else in life besides my survival. I'm inviting you and everybody else to explore this question with me. We're going to eat, have shelter, have clothes. We have achieved survival, yet we live as if we're not going to survive. Not only have we achieved survival, we know that we're going to die. That's an interesting thing, isn't it? Both are true. We have the capacity to live and we will also die. Thought is the denial of both of those things. Thought says you need thought to survive and you'll never die. And by the way, don't think about the contradictions of thought.

Who perceives the limitations of thought? Is thought itself perceiving its limitations or is something else making that perception?

It doesn't seem like that perception can come from thought itself. Thought does not entirely describe life, because there is something when thought is absent. What is this something else?

Thought cannot get to it. Thought can talk about, conceptualize, build systems around it, but it cannot get there, and this is very irritating to thought. This is why we have the churches, the philosophies, and the theologies, because thought is trying to build something as immense as what occurs when thought is absent.

If thought is not everything, then something exists that is not thought-bound, not separate, not me and you, but which is this quality of "us" that we're trying to get to without concepts.

But I'm still in the world of thought, which is telling me if I don't think then I'll die. Faith says, then die, if I have to die. It doesn't make any difference, because I'm dying every moment anyway. In fact I'm going to die physically, so what's the problem with death? It's already happened. Faith says fine, I will face that. I *am* that. I'm not afraid of that. Let's find out, because I know what thought is. I've seen my parents' thought, their parents' thought, a hundred generations of thought. I see the world that thought has created, with all its pain, and I'm not interested in that world as much as I'm interested in what there is to explore.

Now I prepare for my own death. In that preparation, I die. But, magically, I'm still here, you're all still here, even though we just died. Isn't that interesting? Something else begins to occur here. We're not trying to get to that "something else" through thought anymore, that "something else" has gotten to us. The movement is not from thought to consciousness. Instead, consciousness has touched us.

It seems as though a core thought drives those other thoughts. The core thought is that we think we are these bodies. From that core thought we produce the striving and the survival and the victimhood.

The core thought is a fact. The biological thought that this body needs to survive is a fact. However psychological thought can be problematic. Psychological thought can be convinced that the core thought can be sacrificed, as in suicide or war. If we have a righteous reason, we will kill the body.

That core thought is a biological fact, which is that we're alive. Life has its own needs. We breathe, we eat, we love. That core thought is not a problem. When I'm cold, I put on a sweater. When I'm hungry, I eat. That's the basic fact of self. One of the problems with trying to get rid of the self is that we try to get rid of the biological along with the psychological. So we think, "I'm cold, but I'm not really cold. I'm hungry, but I'm not really hungry." I'm then in a confused state in which a lot of crossed signals are going on.

Isn't there a link between biological survival and psychological survival? Don't we think that the survival of "me" is dependent on the survival of the body?

Imagine a world in which we want the body to survive but we aren't concerned with fame, glory, wealth, and prominence. In that world, the distribution of resources would be very simple. If we had no other psychological needs then we would simply be feeding each other, clothing each other, and housing each other.

How does survival of the body become survival of the psychological self? We may be developing as a species. The primitive, reptilian part of our brain may be creating the sense of fear, neurosis, psychology. It may be that we're developing different ways of organizing ourselves physically. As our physical security becomes more evident, the fact is we don't need to be so worried. We live in a culture that is so rich and incredibly secure, and yet most of our time and energy goes into being more secure.

The whole dilemma is based on the notion that we exist outside of ongoing experience. Since that's simply conceptual, there's nothing we can do but be who we are. We have to do nothing.

This is the collapse of the attempt to leave thought. We've been trying to find our way out of thought into this other realm we're calling consciousness or faith. We wanted to see if there may be something that is not thought, something whole.

For a while there, it looked like doing nothing was the access to wholeness or consciousness. Now it is suggested that there's no place to get to other than thought. We're collapsing, crashing back into thought. There's no world of consciousness separate from thought, no world of thought separate from consciousness. There is simply what is. We have no choice, in fact, but to be where we are.

What if that's true? What if there's no choice, nothing to do? We are simply where we are. There's nothing to modify, no way to escape. When we're in hell, we're in hell. When we're in heaven, we're in heaven. Is that the end of the story? Are we just where we are? There's just the now. Can anyone find anything that is not "now"?

We're abandoning all hope and all attempts to modify. If thought takes over now, it takes over in this moment, and this moment, and this moment. As it takes over, it creates the idea that all those moments are in fact interconnected in something called time. The one experiencing those moments interconnected in time is "me." That's what is happening now. Here I am, you're there, and we're both in time.

Is something transformed by the collapse of all of this into now? Thought is generating the sense of time and me and you. It's still churning away. It's still telling us to get better, because we're not good enough. But we don't have any place to go besides where we are. Is that it?

There is an "is-ness" beyond thought.

Is it beyond thought? Because we're suggesting that there's no beyond. There's just what is; there's just what is now.

What I mean is that "is-ness" is not defined by thought. Thought doesn't tell me anything about reality and what is true. This "is-ness" is deeper than thought. It is somewhere that thought cannot take you to.

The "is-ness" you're referring to and the churning, neurotic, self-centered, time-creating thought we've been talking about—are they the same, or are they different?

Where I am now, I cannot relate to churning thought. That doesn't mean that yesterday thought wasn't taking up my attention, but in this moment I feel removed from thought. It is not driving me; it's not what I'm responding to.

But you can still think. What's two times four?

Eight.

I'm glad you didn't ask *me* that. I'm not sure I would have come up with the right answer. So thought is still functioning. In you, thought is multiplication; in someone else it's neurotic process. When you said two times four is eight, was "is-ness" there?

Yes.

There was no battle between thought and consciousness. From the perspective of consciousness, there's no concern about thought. Thought is there. It multiplies, it's neurotic, it's happy, it's sad, it's whatever it is. Consciousness is not really involved with the particular content of thought. It simply attends to it. Now, what is the relationship of thought to consciousness? When we talk about consciousness, do you think, "Do I get that? Am I there?" When thought turns to consciousness, it's very concerned.

Yes. I should have more consciousness; my thinking is probably bad.

You and me both.

We want good consciousness, not bad consciousness, but it is what it is.

This movement from thought to consciousness is hopeless. It can't go anywhere. The movement from consciousness is unconcerned. It's not really concerned with the content of thought. So again we can see thought in all its self-importance really doesn't have much to do with what we're talking about. It can occur in the midst of what we're trying to describe.

What is consciousness? Is it a state of being or an experience of being that is beyond description or thought?

When we talk about consciousness, we're talking about an idea, so we're in the field of thought. Let's be clear about that. Whatever I say about consciousness you can try to incorporate in a philosophical standpoint, or you can look at your own being to discover what it is or isn't. You could say it's the awareness of thought, as well as thought itself; it is everything.

If there are two worlds—the world of thought and the world of consciousness—then when we get to consciousness we can look at thought with equanimity. Whatever thought turns up doesn't make any difference. All we have to do is get out of the world of thought, which is always neurotic. Or are thought and consciousness the same things?

It sounds like consciousness is a state of not having an attachment to good or bad.

That's one of the qualities that seems to be there. When you are aware of anything, you are simply attending to that. There's no sorting. Thought has the quality of sorting. It looks for better or worse, good or bad, because that's part of its technology. That's why we eat the nice ripe apple instead of the wormy green one. It's good to have that discrimination, otherwise we'd be out eating God knows what.

In terms of the relationship between consciousness and thought, it seems pretty clear to me that thought is made of consciousness but that consciousness isn't made of only thought. Consciousness is entirely inclusive, whereas thought is just a subset of consciousness.

If you subtract thought from the universe, do you have consciousness as the remainder? Let's turn it around. Let's take the universe and subtract consciousness, so all you have is thought. Is there a universe? What's there? Look at the Internet. That's actually a very good model of thought without any sort of intelligence. This massive amount of information is burgeoning, exploding, growing, multiplying, self-replicating. There are viruses, life forms. It's a life unto itself, but there's no evidence of intelligence.

What is intelligence? Could we say that it's thought and consciousness slammed together, so that they are integral, indivisible? Don't take my word for this. Look in your own being and see if consciousness infuses thought. When thought arises with consciousness, it is transformed. Awareness-infused thought has a quality of wholeness. It is thought that has a drive, a force, an energy, a direction, a to-do technology, but the perspective isn't me anymore.

Consciousness seems to bring about communion. There's something about it that collects and connects. This world of unity and multiplicity isn't what we described conceptually as unconcerned and in a way disconnected. Nor is it the world of the mind, which is neurotic and involved. There's something else now.

The question is, "How do we investigate this something else?" We started out not knowing. And we still don't know. We thought we knew. We thought we had it down. We thought that the mind was bad, and we had to get to this other place, which was good. We got to the other place and then crashed back into where we are. In that "as-is-ness" consciousness just watched thought—it was so relaxing. But that was also an idea, because consciousness isn't just watching, it's transforming thought. Thought coming in contact with awareness is changed. How can we find out about this? We're still investigating, we still don't know.

Can we become more conscious than we already are? Is there anywhere to get to? Where we are is "now," in which "is-ness" or consciousness is present. Thought may be occurring or not. We start to notice that there are not two things happening in that space, but only one. That, in fact, it is a unitary universe that we could describe as consciousness moving through thought. Not that we're trying to get more conscious, or that we feel less conscious; we don't know anything about that because all we have is the moment to work with. There's no before or after, there's no getting anywhere, there's just this. In this there is something potential or dynamic. It's not an inert universe.

We've graduated from doing nothing. Now we're doing something, but it's consciousness doing something.

We have noticed the movement of consciousness through each of us, which comes about not through our effort, but through the collapse of our effort. Now, the investigation has changed from, "How do I fix 'me'?" to "What is the movement of consciousness? What is it doing?" I am not the doer and you are not the doer, but something is happening.

I am interested in the investigation of the movement of consciousness, the infusion of consciousness, the doing something from consciousness. It occurs in dialogue, in relationship with each of you. So my invitation to each of you is to join me in that living dialogue, which is the experiment of what life can be, just as it is.

What is the potential of now? What is the expression of now? What is the form of relationship, community, education, business, of our entire social and conceptual fabric? This is the question that consciousness appears to be asking as it moves through our world, shatters our world, and reconstructs our world. This is a world of consciousness/thought, a world of intelligence, a world in love, just as it is.

AFTERWORD

It's Beyond Belief

We each must make a discovery in our lives if we are to live in the totality of our human potential. This discovery is very simple and available to each of us, all the time. This realization is that we live in a world that is made up of our concepts, our thoughts, our conditioning.

That is it.

It is a simple realization. It is a profound realization.

Our world is a world of thought that, by its nature, divides what is whole into two. Each thought contains a subject and an object because it contains a thinker and a thought.

Thought, as expressed in language, has become the basis of our individual identities and our social realities. This deeply imbedded schism reflects itself in every word and symbol we use, with the result that we are constantly moving through a series of choices in our lives, the either/or paradigm created, perpetuated, and reinforced by the very structure of our thought process.

This divided viewpoint is destroying us. The division, sorting, and prediction of the world by thought is indeed effective. It builds bridges, it cures diseases, it wins wars. It is a dominating force. But, this is precisely why it does not work. Domination is blind. There are people sleeping under the bridges that thought builds. There are new diseases replacing the ones that thought cures. And, the very winning of war means that war must be waged.

The divided viewpoint is destroying the world we inhabit because it cannot see the whole. The whole is not in thought, it is not in language, and it does not reside in any viewpoint, belief system, or philosophy.

The whole, after all, is all of these and everything else. The whole is what we are. We only think we're not.

As we examine this strange paradox of mind, we find something funny. The inquiry into this conceptual world of separation doesn't bring us to any answers. We cannot find conclusions. We cannot build new thought structures. We observe the division of thought, the illusion of opposites, and in that moment the world collapses into the timeless whole. *We* collapse into the timeless whole.

What will express itself from the whole? How will we live and relate? Can the totality of life, the unindividuated energy of consciousness, infuse all that we are? Can the world that thought built, with its violence, destruction, and chaos—the world of our own minds—suddenly become free from its divisions?

Let us discover this in our lives. Let life discover us.